To: Dad :
From: Dick, Mary, Chris,
Ryan + Charity
July 2002

To: Dad :
From: Dick, Mary, Chris,
Ryan + Charity

Train Stations

DeQUINCY RAILROAD
MUSEUM

KANSAS CITY
SOUTHERN DEPOT

Built in 1923, the depot
an outstanding example
Mission Revival architectu
and is one of the mos
architecturally significa
railroad depots in the sta
Listed on National Regis
of Historic Places.

Train Stations

Whistle Stops, Rail Stations, and Train Depots of North America

by Alexander D. Mitchell IV

COURAGE
B O O K S
AN IMPRINT OF
RUNNING PRESS BOOK PUBLISHERS

Philadelphia • London

Library of Congress Cataloging-in-Publication 2001094410

ISBN 0-7624-1206-7

First published in 2002 by
PRC Publishing Ltd,
64 Brewery Road, London N7 9NT
a member of the Chrysalis Group plc

Published by Courage Books, an imprint of
Running Press Books Publishers
125 South Twenty-second Street
Philadelphia
PA 19103-4399

This book may be ordered by mail from the publisher. **But try your bookstore first!**

Visit us on the web!
www.runningpress.com

PAGE 2: This is the Kansas City Southern Depot in DeQuincy, Louisiana.

Acknowledgments
The publisher wishes to thank the following for kindly supplying the photographs in this book:

© Collection of the New-York Historical Society, negative number 70587, for the front cover photograph;
Tom Kline: 2, 34 (bottom), 39 (bottom), 43, 55, 60 (top), 61, 63, 72 (top) and 73;
© Horace Bristol/CORBIS for pages 5, 7 (top), 11 (top), 19 (top), 31 (top), 49 (top) and 59 (top);
Prints & Photographs Division, Library of Congress for pages 6, 7, 8, 9 (top and bottom), 12 (top and bottom), 18 (bottom),
25, 26 (top), 29 (bottom), 31, 35, 36, 50, 52 and 56;
Alexander D. Mitchell IV for pages 10 (top and bottom), 11, 13, 14, 15 (bottom), 18 (top), 23 (top and bottom), 24 (top),
44, 46, 47, 64, 66-67 (background), 74, 74-75 (background) and 76;
Albert Alecknavage II for pages 15 (top), 17, 20, 22, 36 (background), 37 (bottom), 38, 41 (bottom), 42 (bottom), 62, 70, 71 (top), 73 and 75;
Barry Hollingsworth, Collection of Maryland Rail Heritage Library, Baltimore Streetcar Museum for pages 16 (bottom), 21 (top and bottom),
24 (bottom), 26 (bottom), 27, 28 (top), 29 (top), 32, 37 (right), 48, 54, 65, 67 and the back cover photograph;
Brian Jennison for pages 16 (top), 28 (bottom), 33, 40, 41 (top), 51 (top), 57, 58 (bottom), 68 and 71 (bottom);
Simon Clay for page 30;
Frank Keller for pages 34 (top), 39 (top), 42 (top) and 66;
Ralph E. Edwards, Collection of Maryland Rail Heritage Library, Baltimore Streetcar Museum for page 49;
Joe Greenstein for page 43 (background);
Louis Van Winkle for pages 51 (bottom) and 60 (bottom);
© G. E. Kidder Smith/CORBIS for pages 58-59 (background);
Alexander D. Mitchell IV and H.E. Brouse for page 58 (top).

Contents

< Train Stations >

< 6 >

Introduction

> The railroad station has for over a century and a half played a pivotal but understated role in American life. It has served as the crossroads for the commerce of everyday folk. Over the years, the actual role of stations in a cultural context has changed dramatically. No longer do the vast majority of residents need to know the location of the nearest station to function. They are more likely to memorize highway exits, computer passwords, or the layout of shopping malls instead. The role of the station as a transportation, communications, and commerce center has all but vanished for most people.

Instead, the stations in existence today often act as a touchstone. They represent survivors of an era when spectacular architectural display was the norm rather than an aberration. They hearken back to a time when life moved at a different pace, and people were accustomed to transportation other than their own vehicles. They are often symbolic of an era of history that created their community, or are representative of Victorian, Gothic, or Art Deco architecture, or even rugged pioneer rusticity.

Increasingly, the station is becoming one of the cultural icons of the community. Look at any commemorative print of the historic buildings in a town, or at collectible decorations produced by a town's historical society or chamber of commerce, and the station, past or present, will almost always be there, along with the churches, the firehouse, the schoolhouse, and the town hall. The station's name sign is often carefully preserved or recreated by the community, sometimes with much more care than the more important highway sign at the edge of town, even if trains

LEFT: Deep in the Adirondack Mountains of New York State a "mixed train" (handling both passenger and freight cars) of the Raquette Lake Railway calls at the depot at Eagle Bay, around 1910. The wooden combination depot, built in 1898, survives today, albeit in heavily modified form alongside a road.

BELOW: A passenger train of the Cape Fear & Yadkin Valley RR stops at the depot in the junction town of Bennettsville, South Carolina. The trackage is now operated by the Pee Dee River Railway Division of the Aberdeen & Rockfish RR, but the charming little depot did not survive.

< 1 >

< Train Stations >

ABOVE: The stucco Atchison, Topeka & Santa Fe depot at Gallup, New Mexico was once a lively location during a train stop. Note the "dining room" to the right. The station survives today as a cultural center and a stop for Amtrak trains.

FAR RIGHT, TOP: The Gulf, Colorado & Santa Fe RR (later AT&SF) built this depot in San Angelo, Texas in 1888 when the line reached the city.

FAR RIGHT, BOTTOM: The Northern Pacific RR built this mission-style depot in Bismarck, North Dakota in 1901 to replace the Sheridan House Hotel and depot of 1877. Passenger service ended in 1979, but the station survives today with modifications to its roof.

don't stop there anymore. Original station signs in private hands have been known to command hundreds or even thousands of dollars in the collectors' market.

The syndrome is hardly unique to North America, as railway stations are loved and cherished around the world. But through a combination of geographic diversity, sheer quantity, and architectural variety, the United States and Canada have the richest collection of stations in the world. Thankfully, an amazing number of these stations have been set aside for future generations to use and enjoy, through museum preservation or rebuilding for continued use.

This book would not have been possible without the assistance of many station enthusiasts and photographers across the nation. A great debt is owed not only to them, but also to the amateur historians who have kept and organized data on station history, and the preservationists who have been responsible for the care and maintenance of so many of the stations in the book.

Regrettably, what would have to be considered the grand era of stations has gone. In an era where obsolescence is planned and long-range planning incorporates years rather than decades, many of the projects of the transportation titans of yesteryear appear extraneous, extravagant, and egotistical; no one seems interested in building a railroad, let alone stations of enduring quality. But, as the pages that follow illustrate, we can be glad our predecessors did both. In a sense, stations are enjoying another grand era, finally getting the appreciation long overdue. <

< 8 >

< Introduction >

< 9 >

< Train Stations >

RIGHT: Railroad employee H.E. Brouse poses as a station agent in the handsomely restored agent's office in the Reading RR station at White Deer, Pennsylvania, which was built in 1912. Brouse is a member of the Central Pennsylvania Chapter of the National Railway Historical Society, which operates the office as part of a railroad museum.

BELOW RIGHT & FAR RIGHT: Only minor touches of modernity deface the time capsule of Stewartstown Railroad's station office in Pennsylvania. The station, which was built in 1914, served as the interchange between the Stewartstown RR and the New Park & Fawn Grove RR; a rare interchange between two small "short line" railroads. Basically unaltered for decades, the office and ticket window continue to serve passengers on the railroad's excursion operation.

< 10 >

Chapter 1
The Station in American Life

> In many communities throughout North America, the term "railroad station" may refer to a variety of things. It may conjure the image of the old building in the center of town, both a sparkling architectural gem and an archaic throwback to an earlier era as outdated as the buggy whip. In other places, it may mean the tiny shelter or paved spot along the tracks where a train stops for passengers in the middle of the night. It could be the modern building where commuters board packed trains for their weekday trips to and from the city, or it could even be the best restaurant in town. In yet other towns, it may simply be the name of a street that has not had a station or railroad on it in years. In some cities, the station is now the thriving hotbed of shopping, dining, and fine lodging, bustling with activity like a beehive at most hours. And sometimes it may even have trains passing by, and occasionally stopping to load and discharge passengers.

No matter which image comes to mind, there is no mistaking the place the station occupies in the American psyche. The station, in a social and psychological sense, ranks with buildings like the church, the school, the city hall, the post office, and the library as an icon of community, of place, and of local identity. A 21st-century generation, one likely to have only encountered railroading while sitting at a grade crossing waiting for a seemingly endless train to pass, may wonder how this state of affairs came to be. They may also wonder why a lowly station sign or simple frame building can have an impact on community identity far out of proportion to its cost in wood, brick, metal or paint. Such a generation would be hard pressed to believe

< || >

< Train Stations >

RIGHT: The interior of the Palmer, Massachusetts Depot, complete with arched doorways and semicircular agent's office, is shown as it appeared in 1959. The railroad served the junction of the Boston & Albany RR (a New York Central subsidiary, merged into the NYC in 1961) and the Central Vermont RR. The station survives today as a private business.

BELOW: Save for the gaudy signs boldly advertising the state's ubiquitous native soft drink, this could almost be a train arriving at any station in small-town America at the turn of the 20th century. This is the Atlantic Coast Line RR depot in Valdosta, Georgia in approximately 1920.

that well over 150,000 station buildings of one type or another were dotted around the North American landscape during the peak of railroading in the early 1900s.

For over a century, from the mid-1840s until the 1950s, the railroads of North America played a critical and dominant role in the lives of its residents. Its impact on commerce and day-to-day events in the era is directly comparable to the introduction of indoor plumbing to a later generation, and automobiles, televisions, aviation, and computers in the 20th century. The development and

< 12 >

< Chapter 1: The Station in American Life >

spread of railroading throughout the continent transformed it in ways never fathomed by its inventors, its builders, and its future users. Now, instead of taking days or weeks to cross a state or territory by wagon or carriage, one could travel in mere hours or days to a new or distant region. One group of several men, operating a freight train, could replace hundreds of wagons and their horse teams, or travel enormously faster than a canal boat without being frozen shut in the winter. Five men and an "iron horse" could carry the passengers and cargo of several dozen stagecoaches. Mail and manufactured goods could travel in a matter of days. A farmer, businessman, or merchant could order fine furnishings, manufactured goods, or imported goods from afar and have them shipped to him at an affordable rate, rather than being self-reliant by necessity. The increase in human efficiency made possible by effective transportation is directly observable in the increase in leisure time. The concept of an eight-hour day, rather than ten or 12 hours, became more than a fantasy.

In all of this, the railroad station was the portal between the individual and the network. The agent behind the ticket window was like a purveyor of the wide world beyond the horizon. Through him, one could hear the telegraph click out the news from the next town or another nation. One could purchase tickets to another town on the line, or with the help of huge directories of timetables called *The Official Guide to the Railways* plot an adventuresome journey across the nation by rail. One could arrange for a carload of bricks,

ABOVE: A chartered freight train is used to re-enact a scene from the past at the former Western Maryland Railroad passenger depot at Cumberland, Maryland in September, 2001. The 1913 depot is now used as a visitors' center and ticket office for the Western Maryland Scenic Railroad, which operates over a portion of the former Western Maryland main line to Frostburg.

< 13 >

< Chapter 1: The Station in American Life >

lumber, feed, or coal to be delivered to a town or a loading dock, and a box or flatcar full of cattle or corn could be loaded and shipped to a faraway city.

The outside world came to town via the station in other ways as well. Political candidates barnstormed the state or nation on campaign trains, making speeches to the gathered crowds from the back platforms of the last car. Troop trains carried off soldiers to fight in distant wars. Funeral trains carried the bodies of deceased presidents—among them Abraham Lincoln, William McKinley, Franklin D. Roosevelt, and Dwight Eisenhower—past a mourning American public. Exhibit trains brought (and in some cases still bring) art and museum exhibits to the public, much as a library van brings books to those unable to access such amenities.

The building itself was also an important structure in many parts of the expanding nation. In many communities, the station doubled officially as post office, general store, or community hall, and unofficially as a hangout, a gossip exchange, and a place to watch the world go by. In many frontier towns the station was the first building in town, and assumed a role as the launching pad for further development and settlement. The station's room might serve as a meeting hall, a church, a court room, or a dance hall. And rare was the station without a mascot. A dog or cat, either owned by the

ABOVE: A passenger shelter at Locksley, Pennsylvania, built in 1891, is actually surprisingly typical of the often rudimentary accommodations in rural areas throughout the nation in the early days of railroading. It was formerly a "flag stop" (where passengers hailed an approaching train like a taxi, if the schedule allowed for it) on the Pennsylvania RR commuter line between Philadelphia and West Chester, and was restored by a local historical society.

LEFT: The Rutland RR combination depot in Danby, Vermont, survives today along the Vermont Railway's line between Bennington and Rutland as a private business.

FAR LEFT: The A.M. Groce general store in the village of Muddy Creek Forks, Pennsylvania, built in 1900, doubled as a post office and a station for the Maryland & Pennsylvania RR until the 1950s. It is preserved by the Maryland & Pennsylvania Preservation Society, along with the adjacent mill (with its own freight car dock) and eight miles of railroad line, as a museum.

< 15 >

< Train Stations >

agent, or self-appointed and looked after by friendly railroaders, would be ever present around many railroad stations until modern times.

Despite the fact that railroad stations were private property devoted to serving customers, local residents of a community always referred to the railroad station as "our" station. Ownership, either by continuous patronage of the company or simple civic pride, became assumed in a figurative sense, and citizens were apt to pressure the railroads for a larger station, better facilities, or proper upkeep of "their" station. Many people to this day seem startled to learn that their town does not own the local station, as they once assumed.

The role of the railroad station in American life, though subtle and understated, was nothing short of monumental. Little wonder that so many of the stations now survive as monuments to railroading, to architecture, and to a different era.   <

ABOVE: Boron station was originally located between Barstow and Mojave, California, on the Santa Fe line. It was built in 1896 as a passenger station for Kramer, four miles away, and was moved to Boron in 1941 as a freight depot. After closure it became a museum in 1987.

RIGHT: The Erie RR's 1885 Tuxedo Park depot survived a 1915 train derailment that damaged much of the building, and is still used by commuter trains to and from New York City today. Stucco has replaced the original wooden shingles and siding.

FAR RIGHT: This replica of an original station sign graces the end of a former Philadelphia, Wilmington & Baltimore Railroad suburban passenger station at Glen Mills, Pennsylvania, near Philadelphia. The 1881 brick depot is leased to a local historical society.

< 16 >

< Train Stations >

< 18 >

Chapter 2
The Earliest Stations

> The term "railroad station" refers to more than just a building. Technically, the term signifies a location along a railroad line or track that is designated to serve the handling of its passengers, freight, or services necessary to the railroad (such as fuel, signaling and crew changes). A station can be as little as a patch of gravel along the track with a sign officially marking the location, or it can be a railroad junction with no facilities to service customers. The building universally mentioned when one refers to a "station" is most accurately called a depot. However, many decades of inaccurate use have made the terms more or less interchangeable, and they will be used as such in this book. A terminal, on the other hand, has a more specific meaning; it refers to a station at the end of a major railroad line where trains terminate rather than pass through, although trains sometimes do pass through stations officially referred to as "terminals."

The first railroad depots were almost an afterthought. The earliest railroad lines, developed in the days of stagecoaches, often ran down city streets, and sometimes ticket offices were initially established in adjacent businesses such as taverns or stores. The first city terminal of the first intercity railroad in America, the Baltimore and Ohio Railroad, was little more than a small shed and ticket booth erected at its Mount Clare terminus in western Baltimore, Maryland when horse-drawn services to Ellicott City began in 1830. The paltry terminal was later replaced by a brick building, which still stands as part of the B&O Railroad Museum. The original 1831 stone freight station and engine shed in Ellicott City, Maryland, is preserved as the oldest station surviving in America; the hotel across the street that served as the original passenger station until 1856 also survives. As late as 1866, the Berkeley Hotel (built in 1849) in Martinsburg, West Virginia, was acquired by the B&O to replace a station destroyed in the Civil War. The structure is still used as a passenger station by Amtrak and commuter trains.

As railroads became a certainty rather than a passing experiment or fantasy, more permanent structures were deemed necessary. It

TOP LEFT: The humble brick building in the foreground, built about 1851, stands at the site of America's first railroad station, the Baltimore & Ohio RR's original Baltimore terminus, in the Mount Clare neighborhood of Baltimore, Maryland. Originally a ticket office and office building, it now serves as the main entrance to the B&O Railroad Museum, founded in 1953 in the surrounding buildings and enclosed roundhouse, which were built in 1884.

BOTTOM LEFT: A Baltimore & Ohio train arrives at the railroad's Ellicott City, Maryland, station about 1900. Built about 1831, the original stone freight station received wooden trim and glass windows around 1885. Beyond the station and to the left of the locomotive stands the Patapsco Hotel, the original passenger facility until the 1850s. The depot survives today as a railroad museum honoring America's oldest extant depot.

< 19 >

< Train Stations >

BELOW: *The Pennsylvania RR passenger station at Strafford, Pennsylvania, represents perhaps the most extreme undertaking of wooden Victorian opulence and decoration surviving in an American station today. Now in use as a commuter stop, it was built as the Catalogue Building for the Centennial Exposition in Philadelphia. After the exposition the station was bought at auction by the PRR and moved to Wayne in 1885. In 1887, when the station was moved to Strafford, some of the ornamentation was removed because the station was placed on a sloping piece of land. It now serves as a commuter station for Philadelphia-bound commuter trains.*

also took some time for the developing technology to determine just what form the structures should take. Passengers needed a place to purchase tickets, board the train, and presumably await the train's arrival or departure in comfort. A place was needed to load and unload freight goods, and an agent to collect fees and handle paperwork, among other duties. Depending on the location of the station, the railroad itself had needs to be met by the location. Depots often included a telegraph office to handle the dispatch and control of train movements, perhaps a water or supply stop for the locomotives or livestock cars, and sometimes a place to prepare food for hungry passengers.

Railroads also had different logistical approaches to construction, depending on where the railroad was to be built. A railroad constructed in an established, populated area often had to compromise on the location of its station. The station was situated on the outskirts of the village or wherever land was available. In other cases, such as was often the case in New England, the local topography and the need of a railroad for gentle grades often dictated the location of the town's station a considerable distance from the actual town center. Sometimes this created a separate community of its own. In some places, the only routes available were through less desirable sections of the town—leading to the expression "the wrong side of the tracks." In other cases, the growth in a railroad's traffic eventually made the handling of dozens of trains through the heart of a city or town woefully impractical, forcing the relocation

< 20 >

< Chapter 2: The Earliest Stations >

of the railroad lines to another route outside town or even the other side of a river.

Many early railroad stations in frigid climates were built as giant fully enclosed sheds, much like an oversized barn, with large doorways through which the trains entered to load and unload passengers or freight in relative comfort from the elements. Functionally, the design quickly became obsolete, although a four-track shed and station of this design, built in the 1860s, survived until 1963 on the Central Vermont Railroad in St. Albans, Vermont. The "barn as depot" concept was perpetuated in other early structures, such as those in Syracuse, New York (1838) and Columbus, Ohio (1862). An early terminal of this design, built in 1832 by the B&O in Frederick, Maryland, was not demolished until 1910.

When railroad development reached its zenith in the second half of the 19th century, the presence or lack of a railroad was often deemed critical to the economic development and prosperity of a region. Towns without a railroad might raise the money to build a connecting line to the railroad that had forsaken them to assure their future viability. The valley with a railroad line and stations would often prosper and flourish, while the valley lacking them might stagnate or wither.

In the Midwest and West, however, railroads were very often the pioneering influence, blazing a trail through unoccupied or unsettled areas. Planners for railroads in new territory had the luxury to place stations at their whim and often did it to suit their own needs first, particularly in the case of the Transcontinental Railroad of the 1860s, and Federal land grant programs. In many cases, a railroad station was the first building in town, erected to serve the needs of the advancing railroad and as a stepping stone for settlers.

The design of stations evolved into three basic types, depending on needs. A passenger station served the needs of passengers and railroad staff. Such a station would typically house a ticket window

TOP: The Chesapeake & Ohio RR's depot at Durbin, West Virginia, now a community center, shares touches in common with several C&O stations, including a unique style of decorative wooden trim.

ABOVE: B&O's graceful station in Oakland, Maryland, was built in 1884 to a Queen Anne style design by noted B&O architect E. Francis Baldwin. It replaced a wooden depot which was moved eastwards several miles to Altamont. The distinctive station, last used for passenger trains in the mid-1970s, is still owned and used by the current railroad, CSX Transportation, but is targeted for preservation by the community.

< 21 >

< Train Stations >

BELOW: The Philadelphia, Wilmington & Baltimore RR built its passenger station at Dover, Delaware in 1856. Its successor, the Pennsylvania RR, expanded it in 1911, adding a Georgian Revival façade. It was remodeled again in the 1950s, and then after the end of passenger service on the Delmarva Peninsula in the 1960s was made into judicial offices, a role it continues to serve today.

and agent's office, and at least one waiting room to shelter waiting passengers. Depending on the era and region in which the station was built, it might have a separate waiting room for women and children. The purpose was to spare delicate ladies and youth from the tobacco smoke, spittoons, swearing, or other vulgarities too common to the male gender of the era. In states that practiced racial segregation or "Jim Crow" accommodations, a separate waiting room for blacks, often only accessible via outer doors, might be provided. On a multiple-track rail line, a passenger station usually sat on one side of the line with a small shelter gracing the opposite side of the tracks. In an area served by frequent commuter trains, the station was placed on the side of the tracks where inbound commuter trains stopped, as homebound commuters usually dispersed immediately upon disembarking from their train.

Many early passenger stations also served another role, that of feeding train passengers. Before the development of dining and sleeping cars during the late 1800s, passengers who wished to get a good hot meal or a good night's sleep had to get off a train to do so. In the same way that inns and taverns served travelers on stagecoaches and canal boats, many stations also doubled as restaurants or hotels, where a passenger could disembark to take a bed for the night or attempt to be served and eat a meal during a scheduled meal stop. The scheduled meal stops, however, were typically too short to do justice to a trainload of hungry patrons at once. So places such as the Starrucca House in Susquehanna, Pennsylvania (on the Erie RR, built 1865) and Dodge City, Kansas (on the Santa Fe) sported restaurant depots far larger than the local populace could support in order to cater for hungry train passengers.

< 22 >

< Chapter 2: The Earliest Stations >

LEFT: *Built in 1849–1850, this classical-style building was the original terminal for the Philadelphia, Wilmington & Baltimore RR, which later merged into the Pennsylvania RR. Abandoned in the 1930s and derelict for decades, the building was rescued for preservation by local historians, and renovated as the Baltimore Civil War Museum, opening in 1997.*

BELOW: *The Pennsylvania Railroad's (PRR) station at Lewistown Junction, Pennsylvania, served both the community of Lewistown (across the Juniata River) and the junction of the PRR's main line with a branch into Lewistown and points north. It was opened in 1849 as the westward-expanding railroad reached the area, and survives today as both an Amtrak stop and an archives repository for the Pennsylvania Railroad Technical & Historical Society, dedicated to the original PRR.*

The concept of a dual-purpose station, which also served as a hotel or restaurant, was taken much further by independent businessman, Fred Harvey. In 1876, he started the first of what would prove to be a large chain of independent eateries and hotels in Topeka, Kansas. Known as "Harvey Houses," these operated in railroad stations from Chicago to California, and the Atchison, Topeka & Santa Fe RR were by far his biggest clients. The standards set by the chain were high enough to outlive the development of railroad dining cars and Pullman sleepers, and Harvey Houses lasted into the 1930s. Many of the depots and buildings survive today. A preserved and restored Harvey House restaurant on the old St. Louis–San Francisco Railroad in Hugo, Oklahoma once again serves food, and is now a stop on an excursion train operation.

A freight station, which was built either in a larger community with substantial freight needs or in areas with a great deal of freight originating from it, such as a valley of coal mines or lumber mills, served only the needs of freight customers. Small shipments were delivered to the station to be held for pickup or delivery in a warehouse-style room or shed. Freight cars bearing such shipments were switched into a siding at the station, usually on a regular basis by a "local" freight train from a nearby central yard, or by the line's daily train. Often, adjacent to a freight

< 13 >

< Train Stations >

ABOVE: The Hanover Junction, Pennsylvania, depot, built at the junction of the Northern Central RR and the Hanover Branch RR branch, featured prominently in a noted Civil War era photograph by Matthew Brady's crew, where a tall man in a top hat vaguely appears to be Abraham Lincoln. Closed in 1929, the 1853 depot amazingly survived decades of abandonment and neglect, and is now preserved as a museum and visitor center.

RIGHT: Abraham Lincoln left his home town of Springfield, Illinois in 1861, bound for Washington, from the Great Western Railway depot shown here. Replaced by a passenger and freight station, the Italianate-themed building served for another century as a Wabash Railroad freight office. After a fire in the 1960s, it is now preserved as a private museum to Abraham Lincoln and railroading in Springfield.

station was a public "team track," where carloads of freight could await unloading and pickup by companies with wagons or trucks. The office for the local agent, who handled billing and other affairs for the area's customers, was in the freight house. Freight stations rarely stood alone; they were often placed in conjunction with or adjacent to the same company's passenger station for the community. They were typically far simpler and more utilitarian in design, plainer, and of a less substantial construction. Exceptions abounded of course; the Baltimore & Ohio's freight facilities in Baltimore included a brick warehouse that was 1000ft. (305m) long and eight stories high. It was incorporated into the design of the Oriole Park at Camden Yards baseball stadium in 1992.

Far more common in rural America, and eventually the most common type of station in North America, was the "combination" station, which housed both passenger and freight facilities in one building. Often incorporated under the same roof, usually in a second story, were living quarters for the agent, or the agent and his family. The railroad agent, like a lighthouse keeper, often had his quarters provided by the railroad, but was in return expected to be available virtually around the clock as railroad traffic dictated. The

< 24 >

< Chapter 2: The Earliest Stations >

agent's office, where tickets were sold and paperwork handled, usually separated the freight room from the passenger waiting room. A large number of stations surviving today are the combination form with both passenger and freight facilities.

Whatever form the rail station finally took, a degree of standardization between stations on a company's railroad quickly became the order of the day. Standardization took many forms. Railroads in wealthier, established regions often hired noted architects or their firms to design stations along a commuter line, and often the architect's "signatures" are evident in the buildings to this day. Many companies dictated a color scheme to be used on not only the station, but all affiliated buildings, outbuildings, and even adjacent grain elevators or hotels. Later, larger railroad companies such at the Pennsylvania, the Chesapeake & Ohio, and the Atchison, Topeka & Santa Fe maintained standard blueprints of numerous station designs, and even a ready supply of construction material, ready to build or replace a station on short notice. For this reason it can be easy to find precisely identical stations in different states on the same company's line, or find all the stations on one line built to the same plan or with similar details by a railroad, which was then merged into a larger system.

During the rapid expansion of the West, many stations were thrown together in a temporary or even portable fashion, and a small shed-like structure or even an old railroad car were incorporated into service to start the business functions of the company. As traffic grew, an outmoded station was often dismantled or even placed whole on a railroad car to be shipped further afield. It was then replaced by a larger structure, either a custom structure or one

ABOVE: Nothing depicts the bustle and chaos of a busy railroad junction better than this posed photograph of seven trains at Durand, Michigan's Union Station, where trains of the Grand Trunk Railroad and the Ann Arbor Railroad shared this substantial limestone depot. Built in 1903—shown here just after rebuilding in 1905—it now houses the Michigan Railroad History Museum and an Amtrak train stop.

< 25 >

< Train Stations >

ABOVE: *The Baltimore &*
Ohio's freight station in
Frederick, Maryland, built in
1832, was an example of the
earliest design of railroad station,
the barn-like enclosed porch.
Replaced by a newer station in
1854, it nevertheless survived as a
freight shed until 1910, shortly
after this photo was taken. Note
the doorway for railroad cars to
enter the building to the left,
which is hopelessly small for later
railroad equipment.

RIGHT: *The Canaan,*
Connecticut Union Station, built
in 1872, stood at the intersection
of the Connecticut Western RR
and the Housatonic RR that both
became part of the New York,
New Haven & Hartford RR.
Telegraphers from the two lines
shared the octagonal tower in the
middle of the two railroad wings.
Passenger service ended in 1971,
but the station survived and was
used as a restaurant and offices
for the Housatonic RR.
Tragically, fire destroyed much of
the station in late 2001. It is
hoped at least part of the historic
structure will be rebuilt.

built to another standard design. Oddly, the concept of using a retired railroad car has not disappeared. Even as this was being written, a 1948 Chicago, Burlington & Quincy RR glass-domed stainless steel observation car, the "Silver Horizon," was installed as a depot in Maricopa, Arizona.

The advancement of the telegraph and later the telephone in the mid-to-late 19th century led to their rapid adaptation by the railroad industry. Stations became telegraph offices by virtue of their use in railroad traffic control. Agents received and handed dispatching orders to trains when they stopped, or if the train didn't stop, passed them on by means of hoops of cane or string, which were then snatched by passing train crews. The agent also used signals as a means of communication. Telegraph offices by default became the fastest means of transmission of information and news in America during the first century of railroading. News such as grain and livestock price quotations, disasters, election results, sports' scores, births, deaths, and trial results were transmitted to the world via telegraph agents at stations. For example, much of the nation crowded around telegraph offices to hear the clicks signifying the driving of the Gold Spike to complete the Transcontinental Railroad at Promontory, Utah on May 10, 1869.

Although officially representing the railroad, local residents often saw the railroad station as a local gateway to the outside world. This was in a much more evident manner than the airports that were

< 26 >

< Chapter 2: The Earliest Stations >

LEFT: Located in Massachusetts along one of the two lines that intersect at the Canaan depot, the 1893 Lee depot's unique New England "saltbox" appearance is more the result of accident than design. Originally built by the New York, New Haven & Hartford RR, the station featured a canopy on the trackside, balancing the appearance of the structure. The building is now used as a restaurant. Many other notable depots, including an 1886 depot at Cornwall Bridge and a 1843 hotel-station at Merwinsville, lie along the same line in Western Connecticut.

to succeed them in this role. All manner of raw materials and manufactured goods entered and left town via the railroad lines, such as grain, lumber, coal, dry goods, livestock, automobiles, oil, tractors, steel, and bricks.

Parcel post was not established by the Post Office until 1913, and packages of goods ordered from catalogues arrived via services such as the Adams Express and the Railway Express Agency, which handled freight goods in a manner similar to a parcels or trucking company today. Even coffins carrying the deceased were often shipped to the deceased's hometown and unloaded—with care and dignity—via railroad baggage cars. A great portion of the U.S. Mail was transported via Railway Post Office cars on passenger trains, dropped off and picked up during station stops or even "on the fly" by moving trains.

Many stations doubled as local post offices, and some station agents doubled as postmasters. In many places in America, especially when smaller rail lines were late in coming to a region, a previous general store or post office might serve as the station itself. Several multipurpose stores were built during the late 19th century. Among the survivors is the old A.M. Grove store, which served from 1900 as the station for the fabled Maryland & Pennsylvania Railroad at Muddy Creek Forks, a mill community in Southern Pennsylvania.

The biggest event of the day in many communities was the daily arrival of a train, and many townsfolk would gather to inspect the arrivals and departures of people and things. Small boys were enthralled by the spectacle of the chugging steam locomotive, and would harbor desires of growing up to be an engineer. Newspapers arrived from far-off printing presses, bringing news from around the world. A student or soldier might return home from college, training camp, or the war to an expectant welcome party, or a family of

< 29 >

< Train Stations >

RIGHT: The 1907 stone Grand Trunk RR depot in Gorham, New Hampshire, is now occupied by the Gorham Historical Society, which also displays a steam locomotive nearby.

BELOW: Both the depot and community of Raton, New Mexico owe their existence to the railroad, which operated as many as 60 trains a day through Raton Pass north of the town. The 1904 depot, built to a Spanish Mission style, originally featured spires of red tile rising above the tower. The replacement of steam locomotives by diesels brought an end to most of the rail facilities in town, but the station is still in use today as a passenger station.

immigrants might embark on the final passage to their new homestead, purchased from a far-off agent.

As part of the civic role played by stations, many 19th-century depots were the settings of elaborate landscaping and decoration. Flower gardens (sometimes spelling out the station name in flowers), rock gardens, fountains, shrubbery, and tidy approach lanes were often impeccably maintained at many depots. Sometimes the railroads maintained the landscaping, and even held regional competitions for the best-maintained or most beautiful landscaping. Sometimes the beautification projects were the personal handiwork of the individual agent who lived on the property, or of local residents eager to present a positive face to the world passing by. In other instances, the motives for gardening were of a different nature. The Pennsylvania RR retained greenhouses and gardens around its Gothic brick depot in Newark, Delaware until the 1950s, expressly for supplying cut flowers for its dining cars.

Another innovation of railroading which spread quickly to everyday life was the introduction of "Railroad Time" or Standard Time to the nation. Before the introduction of time zones and a universal time within that zone in 1883, the differences in local time between different cities made the smooth functioning of railroad schedules from east to west or vice versa virtually impossible. High noon in one city would be ten minutes earlier in a town to the west, and the resulting miscalculations in timetables could and did produce catastrophic and fatal results. The railroad industry in a rare act of unity adopted the time zone system to instill uniformity throughout the national transportation network. With the use of fine precision clocks and watches, as well as the synchronization of

< 28 >

< Chapter 2: The Earliest Stations >

clocks via the telegraph system, railroads began operating with a precision never before demanded by the rest of society. As railroads were such a dominant force in American commerce, it was not long before the rest of America set their watches by the station clock, just as future generations would set their watches to radio or television programs.

In the 20th century, another railroad phenomenon evolved which resulted in the construction of more railroad stations. The electric interurban railroad, a hybrid between major intercity railroads and electric streetcars or trolleys developed as electrical technology advanced. The interurban offer a frequent, high-speed connection between urban centers or smaller cities. It showed great promise during its initial days, and both elaborate passenger terminals and small trackside passenger stations sprouted to serve the new technology. Some interurbans also handled modest amounts of parcels or freight traffic, and freight facilities were built to meet these needs as well.

With the unofficial civic role played by railroad stations, it seems little wonder that the local stations of America became local showcases and icons.   <

ABOVE: The Long Island RR depot at East Hampton, New York, epitomizes the Victorian-styled wooden depot. This was very fashionable and popular among several Eastern railroads, including the Reading, Long Island, and Delaware, Lackawanna & Western RRs, during the late 1800s.

LEFT: The Illinois Central RR passenger station at Carbondale, Illinois came with an adjacent "lunch room" for passengers and townspeople alike.

< 29 >

Chapter 3
The Great Terminals

> As both the cities and the railroads of America developed, railroad terminals in the cities evolved into showcases of civic and architectural accomplishment. Many a student of history has referred to these monumental buildings as "cathedrals of capitalism," and whatever the feelings of a viewer towards railroads, it is only one with a cold heart that fails to be awed at the most grandiose of these structures.

Many of the earliest city railroad terminals had little to do with impressing the public, and more to do with establishing connections with ships at harbors or reaching other trade centers. Smoky steam locomotives were often banned from the downtown areas of major cities. It often took several years or even decades before the companies commanded both enough capital and economic clout to construct large terminals closer to the heart of cities.

As the railroad industry grew to become a dominant force in the North American economy, however, access to the railroad became important to the residents of a city. As such, the railroads gradually became the keepers of another standard, that of the architectural grandeur, richness, and occasionally pomposity reserved in earlier times for houses of worship or government.

Styles, such as Italianate, Greek Revival, Elizabethan Revival, Gothic and Art Deco, were reflected in the stations constructed at the time of these architectural fashions. Railroad companies, spending in an outrageously ostentatious fashion, engaged in an unwritten competition of architectural one-upmanship. They began to erect

LEFT: Four years of painstaking renovations were completed in 1998 at Grand Central Terminal, once again exposing the incredible vaulted ceiling showing the night sky painted backward. The famous four-sided, brass clock atop the Information Booth in the center of the main hall is a popular meeting point.

BELOW: Grand Central's exterior, seen here in 1920, is dominated by a 13-foot clock and Jules Coutan's sculpture of Mercury.

< 31 >

< Train Stations >

BELOW: Architects Alfred Fellheimer and Stewart Wagner teamed with design consultant Paul Cret to create Cincinnati Union Terminal in 1933. It took more than three and a half years to construct what is probably the greatest of the Art Deco style railroad stations in the United States.

FAR RIGHT: Portland Union Station, Oregon was opened in 1896. The piling and foundations were put in about 1890, but its completion was delayed by the financial difficulties of the Northern Pacific RR, followed by those of the Union Pacific and later complications with the Northern Pacific. The style of the station and annex is Italian Renaissance and the structure is of pressed brick with gray sandstone trimmings and panels of stucco. It cost $300,000 at the time to build.

increasingly spectacular palaces, dedicated more to their success and might, than to the lowly patron.

The concept of a city terminal as a railway palace began when railroad station buildings moved away from being a barn-like depot consisting of a single building, towards having separate buildings for the office facilities and the tracks. In the 1850s and 1860s, the architectural fashions of the time created what came to be called "railroad style," which consisted of an Italianate villa form with squat squared towers. Examples of this style included: Baltimore's Calvert Station (Northern Central RR, later Pennsylvania RR, built in 1848 and demolished in 1948); Washington, D.C. (B&O, built in 1850 and demolished in 1907); and Gettysburg, Pennsylvania (Hanover Junction, Hanover & Gettysburg, later Western Maryland RR, built in 1858 and still preserved).

The "railroad style," however, soon transformed itself into a wildly eclectic style of its own, mutating into a quirky blend of Italianate, Gothic, Venetian, Romanesque, Greek Revival, Queen Anne, Tudor, Bavarian, Moorish, and could even at times contain Chinese elements. Many of the elements now termed standard to Victorian architecture owe a substantial amount of their heritage to railroad architects of the era, and many surviving stations, particularly those of the Reading RR in Pennsylvania, are classic examples of Victorian architecture. In later years, the builders of larger depots hired architectural firms to draw up unified designs for their stations, drawing once again upon the architectural fashions of the day.

The era of the railroad terminal as a monument, however, was really launched in the 1860s by the New York Central RR, headed

< 32 >

< Chapter 3: The Great Terminals >

by railroad magnate Cornelius Vanderbilt. Inspired by the 1860s construction of the spectacular St. Pancras Station in London, England—itself a pioneer in the railway palace concept—he set about emulating the European tradition with his Grand Central Depot in New York City.

It was designed by architect John B. Snook in the French Renaissance or Second Empire style. The depot, modeled after the Louvre in Paris and completed in 1871 but rendered obsolete by the 1890s, featured separate waiting rooms and facilities for each of the three railroads it served. Passengers transferring between lines had to exit to the street and enter via a separate door—a maddening process that progress and mergers would soon eliminate.

The New York Central quickly outgrew the original Grand Central Depot, and replaced it with an epic new terminal, Grand Central Terminal, started in 1903 and opened in 1913. The Beaux-Arts limestone and granite building would become perhaps the most famous station in America, helped no doubt by the inaccurately named national radio drama "Grand Central Station." But the terminal hardly needed a radio program to promote it. Its main waiting room and concourse featured spectacular arched windows, bronze chandeliers, and marble floors and wainscoting. The main concourse featured an information kiosk, topped by a massive four-faced golden clock, perhaps the most popular meeting place in the city. The ceilings of the concourse depicted a night Mediterranean sky, with thousands of back-lit stars gracing a deep blue sky.

Grand Central Terminal survives today, a plucky survivor in a changing metropolis. It is now overshadowed by the adjacent 59-story Pan Am Building and serves only the passenger trains of the Metropolitan Transit Agency, which secured a long-term lease on the property from the railroad corporation that survived as a real estate company. However, the terminal is a city landmark that is still cherished by its residents. A 1990s restoration of the terminal, which had suffered a lot of dreary modification over the decades, has restored the structure's interior to its former glory once again.

One notable engineering feat pioneered in America at Grand Central Depot and applied to many major terminals to follow was the train shed. A vast, arching roof sheltered the station's many platforms and tracks separately from the depot's waiting rooms and ticket offices. This was the concept of the barn-like train depot taken to extremes. The vast openness of the shed's interior sheltered the passengers and

< Train Stations >

ABOVE AND BELOW
RIGHT: *Nightfall at Denver's*
Union Station, built in 1881 and
expanded in 1894 and 1914–15,
finds trains of both Amtrak and
the Denver & Rio Grande
Western waiting outside the ter-
minal house in March 1983, dur-
ing the last weeks of the Rio
Grande's operation of the Rio
Grande Zephyr *as a non-Amtrak*
passenger train.

trains, but allowed smoke to drift upwards and away. Their span continued to increase in size and reached their zenith in Philadelphia. The Reading Terminal of the Reading RR opened in 1893 with a shed that spanned 256ft. (78m), and the simultaneous expansion of the Pennsylvania RR's 1881 Broad Street Station nearby incorporated a single span of 300ft. (91m).

Train sheds were not without their problems, however. They were noisy chambers, impossible to clean and subject to corrosion and leaking. They were even fire hazards, as the Pennsylvania RR discovered in June 1923 when fire swept its majestic Broad Street Station, reducing the train shed to a steel skeleton which was later demolished. A practical alternative arose in 1906 when Lincoln Bush installed a new design of shed at the Delaware, Lackawanna & Western RR's new railroad and ferry terminal in Hoboken, New Jersey. The new design was arched from the center of platforms serving two tracks, with each arc spanning an adjacent track and half the platform, meeting with another arc between the two adjacent tracks. Skylights provided illumination, and a slot directly above the steam locomotive smokestacks vented smoke to the skies. Several stations were built to this design, later called the "Bush Shed" for the inventor's patent, before an even simpler design took hold. "Umbrella" or "butterfly" sheds simply sprung two roof wings over the platforms from central support poles. Although far less expensive than the huge train shed, the new design also offered far less protection from the elements to the passenger.

< 34 >

< Chapter 3: The Great Terminals >

Another factor that affected station design was legislation, passed in certain cities, that banned the use of steam locomotives in certain areas and mandated the use of alternate means of propulsion to eliminate smoke hazards. In 1895, the first electric locomotive system was developed for the Baltimore & Ohio RR's new Mt. Royal Tunnel in Baltimore. Similar electrification systems, spurred by legislation or operational efficiency, spread to many urban railroads. Most notably these were underground and elevated transit systems, but the New York Central, New Haven, Pennsylvania, and Delaware, Lackawanna & Western railroads (all in the metropolitan New York City region), the Illinois Central RR in Chicago, and the Canadian National in Montreal also had electrification systems.

Electrification was also an integral part of the interurban railroad concept of the early 1900s. A vital advantage of electrification was that it made long underground tunnels feasible to and from underground platforms at city stations, freeing up vast amounts of valuable inner city real estate formerly occupied by tracks for development or sale. Electric "third rails," which often supplied electricity to the cars in transit systems and many railroad systems, mandated the use of high-level platforms. From platforms that were higher up, passengers could board at the car's floor level instead of from ground level via steps at the car's doors.

Eventually, the constraints of finances, available real estate, rationalization, and governmental orders forced many former rival railroads to consolidate operations in a joint terminal. These depots, called "union stations," could serve two or more railroads in a common facility, often administered by an independent corporation

ABOVE: The Terminal Station in Atlanta, Georgia, built in 1905—shown here in 1910— served the Central of Georgia, Atlanta & West Point, Seaboard Air Line, Southern, and Atlanta, Birmingham & Atlantic Railroads. The city's Union Station served the Atlantic Coast Line, Louisville & Nashville, Nashville, Chattanooga and St. Louis, and the Georgia Railroad. The baroque-style structure lost its two towers after a lightning strike shortly before World War II. The structure was demolished in 1972; an office building and rail yard occupy the site today.

< 35 >

< Train Stations >

RIGHT: *Philadelphia Broad Street Station opened in December, 1881. A large train shed covered the stub-ended tracks atop a retaining wall, known throughout Philadelphia as the Chinese Wall because of its resemblance to the Great Wall of China from the street below. It was demolished in 1953.*

BELOW RIGHT: *The Pennsylvania RR's 30th St Station, Philadelphia, was the fourth railroad station to occupy the site. The design of 30th Street Station in 1933 took a radically different approach from that of Broad Street Station. It had tracks that passed under the station, something made possible by the advent of the electric locomotive. The arrangement permitted the routing of trains in a through pattern without the need to reconfigure the engine and cars.*

FAR RIGHT: *St. Louis Union Station is a massive Romanesque-style building, designed by architect Theodore Link in 1894. It was once the busiest railroad terminal in the world. In 1976, the Station was designated as a National Historic Landmark. After an extensive restoration the facility reopened in 1985. The Grand Hall features a barrel-vaulted ceiling of unsurpassed gilt work and has stained glass over the entrance.*

owned by the participating railroads. Union stations served cities as large as Chicago, which was built between 1913 and 1925 and served four railroads. They also served places as small as Canaan, Connecticut, where two intersecting lines shared an L-shaped depot built in 1872, and Selma, North Carolina, where another L-shaped building, built in 1924 and still in use, served the Atlantic Coast Line and Southern Railway.

St. Louis Union Station, which opened in 1894 (replacing a Union Station of 1875) and one of the largest and busiest railway hubs on the continent at the time, outdid them all in size and grandeur. Its five-span train shed, 606ft. (184m) wide, 630ft. (192m) long, and 75ft. (23m) high, covered 10 acres, thirty tracks, and 3.5 miles (5.6km) of sidings serving six railroads. (Even that would prove to be inadequate, and the sheds were lengthened to 810ft. (246m) in 1903.)

Abutting the sheds was a massive medieval, castle-like head-house, designed by St. Louis architect Theodore C. Link. It incorporated a huge Grand Hall full of stained glass, mosaics, marble, and bas-reliefs. At its height in 1920, the facility saw an average of 269 trains a day, and unlike other stations with high train numbers

< 36 >

< Chapter 3: The Great Terminals >

in the era, almost none of the trains in question were commuter trains, but long-distance trains.

The beauty of a union station went far beyond the architectural details of, for example, the Beaux-Arts Washington [D.C.] Union Terminal (opened in 1907), the openness of Kansas City Union Station (1914), or the Romanesque and Queen Anne styling of the red brick Portland Union Station, Oregon, (1896). In a Union Station, travelers and their baggage could swiftly and conveniently change trains from one railroad to another, or change from a commuter train to an intercity train, without crossing town to another terminal. The construction of a Union Station, however, also brought an immediate or gradual end to a lot of older city terminals, many of which were themselves architectural gems. Among these were the 1851 Italianate B&O depot and the 1873 neo-Gothic Baltimore & Potomac (later Pennsylvania RR) depots in Washington, D.C.

The concept of a union station continued to evolve throughout the 20th century. Efforts continued in several cities to consolidate railroad operations in one station, often with mixed results. In Buffalo, New York, a rail gateway to Canada and the Midwest, the eight major railroads operating through the city like a maze, never managed to agree to terms for a union depot. However, two of the more spectacular success stories were in Ohio. In Cleveland, a new

< Train Stations >

RIGHT: Concurrent with the construction of 30th Street Station, the Pennsylvania RR also built Suburban Station in 1930 to begin the replacement of Broad Street Station. A complete contrast stylistically, the building more closely resembles an Art Deco storefront or skyscraper of the era.

FAR RIGHT, TOP: The Union Pacific RR's station in Salt Lake City, Utah, built 1909 in a French Renaissance Revival style, features two murals by San Francisco artist John A. MacQuarrie. Above the main waiting room is Driving the Golden Spike, *depicting the completion of the Transcontinental RR in nearby Promontory in May 1869. The depot is now in use as an arts museum and arts council office.*

FAR RIGHT, BOTTOM: A classic neon sign, sadly in need of repair, hangs outside a restaurant at Denver Union Station in 1990. The steam trains of the type depicted on the sign yielded to bigger and newer steam locomotives in the early 20th century and later to diesel trains.

underground terminal was begun in 1919 and opened in 1930. The new station consolidated operations of the New York Central, Erie, Baltimore & Ohio, and New York, Chicago & St. Louis ("Nickel Plate") Railroads, as well as electrified rapid transit lines to the suburbs (the latter being built by the Nickel Plate's owners). The terminal was topped with a 52-story skyscraper, which dominated the city's skyline. Underneath were station concourses lined with marble, columns, and murals, and four acres of shops and restaurants, managed by the Fred Harvey Company of "Harvey House" fame.

Cincinnati Union Terminal, opened in 1933, became not only one of the last major union stations built, but one of the greatest; an Art Deco masterpiece of world renown. Seven railroads finally agreed in 1927 to consolidate their widely scattered operations, and construction began in 1929—just before the stock market crash in October of that year—at a location nearly a mile west of downtown. New York architects Alfred Fellheimer and Stewart Wagner had Philadelphian designer Paul Philippe Cret refine their original designs into a massive rotunda with a concrete and steel half-dome fronted by a glass, marble, and limestone facade. In front of this main entrance was a plaza with fountains and a reflecting pool and approach driveways. Below and behind the entranceway were ticket offices, shops, a newsreel screen, murals, 16 mosaics, avant-garde décor that included neon and natural lighting and pastel

< 38 >

< Chapter 3: The Great Terminals >

< 39 >

< Chapter 3: The Great Terminals >

themes, underground parking garages, and even provisions for an aviation runway and rapid transit lines (neither would be used).

Los Angeles is in territory stereotyped as having a love affair with the automobile, so it may seem perhaps strange that the last of the great union stations of the old era would be built there. The delay in its construction, like many other late union stations, was because of disputes and bickering between the intended tenants—the Santa Fe, Union Pacific, and Southern Pacific RRs. The depot, which opened in 1939, blended an overall Spanish flavor (after all, the site was next to the city's original Spanish Plaza) with Art Deco detailing and finishes, and was constructed of steel and concrete. A large post office terminal adjoined the complex, as did ample parking, a rarity for railroad stations of the time. Regrettably, the terminal would be woefully underutilized throughout the years. Only in the 1990s did commuter train traffic augment the thinning ranks of intercity passenger trains. The terminal never lost its glamour, however, as movie stars and the celebrities of Hollywood continued to use the first-class trains as long as they could be considered a first-class operation.

The concept of a union depot would prove to be a good one even in the modern era. In the 1980s, Amtrak (the national passenger train operator described in more detail later) undertook massive reconstruction of a derelict freight rail line to connect former New York Central rail lines to its Pennsylvania Station. This eventually united all of its operations in New York City in one facility and rendered New York City's landmark, 1913, Beaux-Arts Grand Central Terminal to commuter terminal status.

ABOVE: The Los Angeles Union Passenger Terminal,was completed in 1939, well into the automobile age and shows a Spanish and Art Deco blend of architecture.

LEFT: Although Pennsylvania Station in Baltimore, Maryland, was named for the railroad that built it, it also served the Western Maryland RR. The 1911 French Renaissance building, designed by Kenneth Murchison, succeeded two earlier Union Stations built in 1873 and 1886. Today the pink granite structure is still used to serve passenger trains.

FAR LEFT: The Santa Fe station in San Diego, California, was constructed to the classic Atchison, Topeka & Santa Fe mission style in 1915, and was nearly demolished in the 1960s. The waiting room features long oak benches and magnificent bronze chandeliers.

< 41 >

< Train Stations >

RIGHT: *The Spanish Colonial flavor of the 1927 Atlantic Coast Line passenger station in Orlando, Florida is said to derive from architect M.A. Griffith's forays to the American Southwest before designing a station in what was also originally a Spanish colony. It was used later by the Seaboard Coast Line and Amtrak, and was renovated by local volunteers in the early 1990s.*

BELOW: *Railroad magnate Cornelius Vanderbilt's Grand Central Terminal in New York City was completed in 1913 and is still a celebrated landmark of the city today.*

The era of the distinctive and monumental unified station did not end with the establishment of union stations. Enough railroads with a sense of grandeur or largess survived in cities with no serious competition in the 20th century to build further grand stations. Most, such as the Cincinnati Union Terminal, were conceived and begun during the 1920s, an era of financial prosperity that could be regarded as the railroad industry's last great hurrah. Some of the later stations, particularly in the West, were upgraded stations to accommodate ballooning populations due to the western migration of Americans. Among these were the 1926 Southern Pacific depot in Reno, Nevada (the fourth on the site) and the 1925 Union Pacific RR Spanish Colonial Revival depot in Boise, Idaho, which was only built when a through line was created through the state capital.

The Pennsylvania RR, seeking to streamline its operations in and through Philadelphia, constructed two terminals in the city and opened the downtown Suburban Station in 1930 and the outer-downtown 30th Street Station in 1933. The two stations were a sharp study in contrasts.

Suburban Station, designed to replace Broad Street Station a block to the east, was a precursor of things to come. An underground terminal and concourse covering 12 acres was covered with a classic Art Deco office building, 20 stories in height, designed by the Chicago firm of Graham, Anderson, Probst, and White. Rather than grand facades and high ceilings, the station's entrance

< 42 >

< Chapter 3: The Great Terminals >

more closely resembled a storefront of the era, and led to a subterranean shopping complex and ticket offices. Oddly, in spite of the efficiency and convenience of the modern terminal, Broad Street Station was not closed until 1952. Suburban Station's platforms and tracks were effectively a dead-end tunnel; the city would eventually undertake to extend the tunnel and connect its commuter traffic to the former rival Reading RR commuter network, a task it would complete in 1985.

Meanwhile, along the banks of the Schuylkill River, an enormous neoclassical temple, 30th Street Station, arose like the Parthenon of Athens. Standing at the end of Market Street's downtown district, the major terminal with a name like a subway station featured porticoes facing east and west with 70ft. (21m) Corinthian columns. The station, serving hundreds of trains a day, served as one of the most complex junctions in Eastern railroading, perched in a triangle of lines stretching north to New York, south to Baltimore, and west to Harrisburg. Through trains arrived and departed on the many platforms below the main concourse, and suburban commuter trains served an upper-level concourse. Like many other cities, the station gradually became tired, neglected, and taken for granted by the locals. In 1988–90, Amtrak, now the owner of the station, undertook a restoration project that amounted primarily to a thorough cleaning of the exterior's limestone and the interior's marble, gilding, bronze, and statuary. Side concourses that had long since been closed and ticket windows were rehabilitated and reopened, and new commercial development solicited. The effect was stunning, showing Philadelphians a structure they had probably never seen before, one that was fresh, alive, and thriving.

Although the grandeur of the large railroad stations are throwbacks to an era and a philosophy that will likely never reoccur, we can take a degree of comfort that the railroad companies did "build for the ages." Can anyone, in retrospect, possibly foresee the eventual preservation of an aging austere bus depot or sterile airport terminal?   <

BELOW: A beautiful stained-glass window makes a striking feature in the interior of the station in San Antonio, Texas.

< 45 >

Railroad Signal Towers

> A structure related to the railroad depot, but serving a different function, is the railroad signal tower, also referred to as an interlocking tower or signal box. The railroad tower is a structure, almost always at least two stories high, in which railroad staff control, by mechanical or electrical means, track switches and signals in an immediate area, such as a junction, station, or switching yard.

In order to facilitate the smooth, non-stop operation of trains from one track to another, switch tenders were assigned in the early days of railroading to set track turnouts for the train's desired route. These were at junctions or the ends of passing sidings. It took very little time for mechanical ingenuity to take over, and before long a single man could set multiple switches via a system of levers, rocker arms, and rods. In order to command a good view of the environment, the switch lever mechanisms were eventually raised in an enclosed platform, which evolved into the tower form.

The inventions of telegraphy and telephones were integrated into the operation of switch towers to facilitate traffic control. Morse code and voice communications were supplemented by electro-mechanical signaling systems, designed to prevent two trains from occupying the same track at the same time.

Another development, which vastly increased the safety of moving trains, was the "interlocking" system. Originally, interlocking systems were complex mechanical linkages, custom designed for each location. They ensured that switches and signals could not be set in such a manner as to allow a collision or other accident to occur, or to indicate a "clear" signal until the switches or signals were set properly. Later, interlocking systems became electro-mechanical, and later still all-electric systems performed the same functions. Similarly, the rod-and-lever mechanisms were replaced by pneumatic and electric switch mechanisms to throw the track switches remotely. Interlockings would range from small locations with only a dozen or so levers or switches to massive, sprawling buildings with teams of men operating hundreds of levers or switches in a carefully calculated cacophony.

Station agents were occasionally capable of operating switch levers from within a station. Far more often they only controlled train order signals, which indicated to a train crew whether the station had telegraphed orders from a central dispatcher to pick up. The "semaphore" signal arms seen protruding from many a station's roof or bay window are train order signals. Switches, and the associated interlocking towers, were usually set a distance from the station, as trains typically would change tracks if necessary before or

LEFT: The former Baltimore & Ohio RR "HO" Tower is one of the last all-mechanical towers in the nation as it stands during the night across the river from Hancock, Maryland, awaiting its eventual decommissioning. It was opened in November 1901 and "modernized" in 1912. The rods in the left foreground are part of the mechanical linkages connecting the levers in the tower to the track switches.

< 45 >

< Train Stations >

ABOVE: Built in 1894, Hunt Tower stood along the Pennsylvania RR in Huntingdon, Pennsylvania and guarded an interlocking that included the junction with the Huntingdon & Broad Top Mountain RR. Removed from service by Conrail in the 1980s, the tower was preserved by the Huntingdon County Transportation Society and is preserved as a museum.

after a station stop. Some towers, however, shared the same property plot as the depot. Part of the operational division was also due to the fact that agents and switchmen on larger railroads often belonged to different unions, and therefore received different pay rates and assignments.

Interlocking towers would become a sure and easy victim of automation and technological advances. The same electrical controls that threw a particular switch or signal from 50ft. (15m) away could, with proper wiring, be just as easily controlled a mile or thousands of miles away. Beginning with the reductions in traffic after World War II and the concurrent developments in electrical components and computerization, traffic control on the railroads was slowly consolidated and centralized, signal by signal, tower by tower, and region by region. Today, most major railroads are controlled by centralized dispatching centers, often in bunker-like buildings nowhere near a track or railroad line, that control movements over entire divisions or an entire railroad.

A few installations defied modernization for years, however. The massive, sprawling interlocking outside the Pennsylvania RR's 30th Street Station in Philadelphia was named "Zoo" after the nearby Philadelphia Zoo, but anyone who worked there alleged the complex "spaghetti bowl" of tracks and switches named the tower instead! Popular legend said that various attempts to automate the tower's functions came to grief when the computers that were used to consolidate the data crashed, or it was claimed that the operations required from the tower were functionally impossible. Nevertheless, an army of operators mastered the fine art of keeping traffic moving through the junction until the 1980s.

From a high of tens of thousands of towers at the turn of the 20th century, it is estimated that less than 120 towers operated in North America in the year 2001. Many were technically drawbridge tender stations, used to control railroad drawbridges by visual contact. A great many of the others were concentrated around complex inter-railroad junctions and crossings in the Chicago area, and even those were closing one by one. The last stretch of main line railroad in the United States to feature a series of functioning interlocking towers in the old fashion—complete with manual levers and rod mechanisms—was, ironically, a stretch of the pioneering railroad in the U.S., the Baltimore & Ohio. As of the end of 2001, a handful of towers still lined the former B&O tracks of CSX Transportation between Baltimore and Pittsburgh, awaiting their replacement circuitry to be cut in so they could be retired. Another tower, a Victorian-trimmed relic, remained in operation in Altoona, Pennsylvania on the former Pennsylvania RR, awaiting retirement and possible preservation. Many other towers lie abandoned and derelict along active and former rail lines, particularly brick and

< 46 >

< Chapter 3: The Great Terminals >

concrete ones, although most towers retired recently have been demolished immediately upon retirement.

Tower preservation is rarer than station preservation, but successful efforts have been made. A wooden Pennsylvania RR (PRR) tower from Lemoyne, Pennsylvania, J Tower, was dismantled in 1984–5 and moved to the Strasburg Railroad excursion line for preservation. Another wooden tower of the B&O's surviving family, the already retired Miller Tower, has been dismantled and moved to Martinsburg, West Virginia for eventual reassembly and restoration. Other towers have been preserved at Bowie, Maryland (a PRR tower in town, moved away from the tracks) and Sykesville, Maryland (a PRR tower from outside the Baltimore station, dismantled and reassembled near the town's B&O station restaurant). Another PRR tower, the brick 1929 Harris Tower, is preserved at its original site by a Harrisburg rail enthusiast organization, and 100 rail miles (160km) to its northwest stands "Hunt" Tower, another preserved brick tower. Other recently preserved towers are in Flatonia and Dallas, Texas; Harrington, Delaware; Terre Haute, Indiana; and Oakland, California.

In an age where temperature controls can be set on individual railroad refrigerator cars by satellite, and individual cars traced by lineside radio tag detectors, the survival of interlocking towers can be viewed in two ways. It is either due to the extreme backward contrariness of a conservative railroad industry, or simply the refusal of dinosaurs to be slain.   <

BELOW: An Amtrak train rockets past the former Pennsylvania RR Bell Tower, which was built in 1904 and overlooks a series of crossovers on the busy Philadelphia–Washington line just northeast of Wilmington, Delaware. It was abandoned in the 1980s.

< 4] >

Chapter 4
Decay and Decline

> Two key events led to the decline of railroading, and the original role of the station, as a part of everyday life in North America during the 20th century. These were the development of motorized road transport, and the later development of the highway network.

Motorized road vehicles, developed during the later part of the 19th century and elevated to mass production and distribution between the two world wars, struck a double blow to railroads. First, the option of personalized transport was too rich an enticement for freedom-loving Americans. No longer need a person be a servant to the schedules of the railroad or interurban; one could just start up a car or truck and drive into the city or directly to a business or residence. Instead of loading a box car that would take several days or weeks to travel to a track at or near its destination, one could just as easily load a truck to drive directly to a loading dock or farm in only hours or days.

The enormous government investment in the roadway infrastructure of America during the first half of the 20th century, and the creation of the Interstate Highway System that began in 1956, effectively sealed the fate of railroading as the major transport mode in the United States. Beginning after World War I and continuing through the century, passenger train ridership went into a precipitous decline. Rail lines that had several passenger trains in each direction during World War I lost all passenger trains before World War II and few interurban electric railroads were to last long either.

Gasoline rationing and military traffic during World War II sparked a dramatic upsurge in rail traffic, but the postwar economy of the 1950s saw the sharpest decline yet. Flagship first-class and express trains disappeared to be replaced by trains of coaches that acted as

LEFT: Louisville, Kentucky's Union Station, built in 1891 and rebuilt after a 1905 fire, was owned by the hometown railroad, the Louisville & Nashville, and used by the Pennsylvania RR and Monon RR. The trainshed was demolished in 1973, and the building saw its last passenger train in 1978. Amtrak passenger trains returned here in 2001.

BELOW: The White Top Station, Virginia, of the Norfolk & Western RR, seen here in 1956, was the highest point served by a regular railroad east of the Mississippi River at 3,585ft. (1,092m). Abandoned by the railroad in 1980, the station was rebuilt as a visitors' center on the Virginia Creeper bicycle trail.

< 49 >

< Train Stations >

BELOW: *The Atchison, Topeka & Santa Fe RR's Grand Canyon, Arizona, depot was built in 1910 to serve the railroad's 1905 El Tovar Hotel, the luxury hotel seen to the rear. The station designed by Francis Wilson, used local Ponderosa pine in a log-slab rustic style evocative of the hotel and log cabins. Abandoned by the railroad in 1968 and acquired by the National Park Service in 1982, it found a new life when the Grand Canyon Railroad initiated passenger excursion service between the canyon and Williams in 1989.*

"jacks-of-all-trades," making every stop. The only reason that as many passenger trains survived was mostly due to U.S. Mail contracts that handled bulk intercity mail on passenger trains. Many passenger trains made more money from the mail handled in the baggage or RPO cars than from the total revenue from passengers. In 1967, however, most railroad mail contracts were canceled and the traffic switched to trucks. The result was that America was in grave danger of losing all of its intercity passenger trains as the losses mounted on the bottom lines of railroad ledgers.

The formation in 1971 of the federally funded (but quasi-public) National Rail Passenger Corporation, or Amtrak, to assume operation of intercity trains in the United States would assure at least a degree of survival for long-distance passenger train travel. However, the cuts in service were still of an almost Draconian nature, and nearly half of the previous routes and trains were eliminated upon the startup of Amtrak. In Canada, a similar agency, known as VIA Rail, was formed in 1977 to assume Canadian intercity passenger operations. About the same time, local transit agencies in major metropolitan areas such as Chicago, Boston, Toronto, and Philadelphia began to assume direct control of regional commuter trains. This started with managing the equipment and personnel and later by taking over ownership and maintenance of the rail lines themselves, including the stations.

Meanwhile, the freight side of railroading also suffered dramatic change during the century. The development of a national highway system facilitated the development of an expansive trucking industry. The expansion in truck traffic coincided in part with the Great Depression of the 1930s, striking a double blow to the fortunes of

< 50 >

< Chapter 4: Decay and Decline >

the railroad industry. After the 1950s, the American economy also shifted from a production economy to a service economy, necessitating the haulage of less raw and bulk materials and more finished, high-value goods. Traffic patterns also shifted. For example, the coal mines of the Appalachians were displaced by the "Powder River Basin of Wyoming" as the nation's largest originator of coal trains. Mergers also swept the railroad industry, resulting in, among other things,

the disastrous merger of the Pennsylvania and New York Central Railroads in 1968.

By the 1980s retrenchment and bankruptcies had led to the formation of the Consolidated Rail Corporation (Conrail) in 1976 to bail out and merge six major Northeastern railroads. The western half of the Chicago, Milwaukee, St. Paul, & Pacific RR was abandoned in early 1980, and the Chicago, Rock Island & Pacific RR was dissolved later in 1980. Merger mania would continue until by the end of the 20th century there were only six major railroad corporations in the United States and Canada, along with a multitude of regional and "short line" operators. Over the course of the century, the railroad industry would be forced to refine its mission from a common carrier serving every freight and passenger need to a

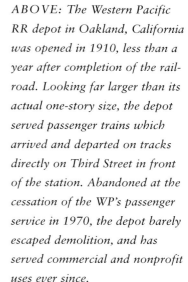

ABOVE: The Western Pacific RR depot in Oakland, California was opened in 1910, less than a year after completion of the railroad. Looking far larger than its actual one-story size, the depot served passenger trains which arrived and departed on tracks directly on Third Street in front of the station. Abandoned at the cessation of the WP's passenger service in 1970, the depot barely escaped demolition, and has served commercial and nonprofit uses ever since.

LEFT: The towers of the 1906 Grand Trunk Railroad (later Grand Trunk Western) in Battle Creek, Michigan were originally topped with Hindu-style domes, adding to the rich mixture of styles and material in the granite and brick building. The depot was used by the railroad for years after the discontinuance of passenger service in 1971. The station was privately redeveloped in the late 1980s but is still used as an Amtrak stop.

< 51 >

< Train Stations >

< 52 >

< Chapter 4: Decay and Decline >

specialized transport industry concentrating on the efficient transport of bulk goods and trainload lots over long distances in an efficient manner.

Other technological progresses had their effects on the railroad station. The development of the telephone network, two-way train radio communications, and improvements in signal and traffic control technology rendered the dispatching, billing, and telegraphing duties of local agents obsolete. Computerization and centralization of merged railroad systems eliminated the jobs of thousands of freight agents, already in jeopardy from the decline in the number of customers. The conversion of railroads from steam locomotives to diesel locomotives eliminated the need for many servicing facilities, such as the water tanks that often shadowed many an old station. In short, huge numbers of railroad stations across the nation were rapidly losing their reason to exist.

Furthermore, high maintenance costs, and enormous tax bills often jeopardized large city stations. Large freight houses were replaced by parcel services, and carload freight stations by facilities built specifically to load trailers, automobiles, foodstuffs, or steel on railroad cars. Grandiose passenger terminals such as Philadelphia's Broad Street Station and Reading Terminal, or San Francisco's Southern Pacific Station, were hardly necessary to serve the needs of weekday commuters. Los Angeles Union Passenger Terminal didn't even have commuter trains. Nor did a consolidated transit agency or Amtrak need multiple terminals in a city, especially when subways were being expanded to suburban areas, and the downtown areas of major cities became decreasingly important as an employment hub. Efforts began to consolidate operations by uniting rail lines into the better or best of two or more stations, often with the construction of connecting tracks between once-competing railroads. In Philadelphia, the two separate commuter rail networks of the PRR and Reading were eventually connected by means of a tunnel and an underground station that replaced the Reading Terminal (later converted into a city convention center).

As formerly bustling halls turned into echo chambers, many railroads went into a retreat mode. They attempted to find buyers for their massive "white elephants," while restricting passengers to modest or tiny facilities, or corner rooms to buy tickets and wait for trains. By the 1950s and 1960s, it was obvious by the actions of many railroads that they were actively discouraging passengers to use trains. If passenger traffic was decreased enough they could appeal to state or federal regulators to discontinue non-profit making services.

Washington Union Terminal, in the nation's capital, suffered a more indignant fate. In the late 1960s, an attempt was made to convert the cavernous expanse of the 1907 terminal into a National

LEFT: The small retail establishments and shopping centers that cluttered the floor of Pennsylvania Station in New York City detracted from the classical architecture of the building before its closure and demolition. Retail installations in stations, such as Washington Union Station, are now more sympathetic to the preceding architecture. Note the early digital clock in the middle of the hall, contrasting with the two classic analog clocks.

< 55 >

< Train Stations >

BELOW: The Union Depot in Mobile, Alabama was built in 1907 by the Southern Railway and the Gulf, Mobile & Ohio Railroad. The spectacular Spanish Colonial Revival structure, topped with an octagonal dome and decorated with baroque-style sculptured trim, was last used for passenger trains in 1958, and is seen here while still occupied by railroad offices. A highway now cuts directly in front of the station, which is vacant and difficult to access.

Visitors' Center for the nation's Bicentennial celebration in 1976. The project was never fully completed, going far over budget, and closed the station's Main Hall to the public in 1981. Train and subway passengers were shuffled off through crude construction passages to access their trains.

The fate that awaited the Central Terminal of Buffalo, New York, was almost as bad. It was opened in 1930 after the city's eight railroads could not agree on terms for a union station, and was a masterpiece of Art Deco. It had open plazas, a 271ft. (83m) office tower looming over a 450ft. (137m) concourse, and a 360ft. (110m) baggage and mail wing. The grand concourse featured marble ticket counters, terrazzo flooring, and vaulted ceilings. Unfortunately, the station was cursed with a location two miles from the center of town, and was for the era psychologically similar to an airport located far from the city today. Traffic never reached expectations, and the station quickly became a white elephant to a New York Central management that was noted for its anti-passenger outlook. It was put up for sale in 1956, but languished until a buyer came forward in 1979. Unfortunately that buyer lost the building to a tax auction, and the derelict and vandalized ruin has been a source of soreness and contention between owners and local officials ever since. In 1979, Amtrak abandoned the station for the New York Central's Exchange Street Station (built in 1952).

Other classic stations were also lost to consolidation or redevelopment. Milwaukee's 1886 Union Station was slated for demolition and replacement in the 1960s; a fire gutted the brick structure

< 54 >

< Chapter 4: Decay and Decline >

before demolition began. In its place rose a concrete and glass box-like structure, still in use today. The nearby Chicago & North Western station, built in 1889 on the Milwaukee waterfront, was unluckier still. It was razed in 1968 for a highway ramp that was never even built. Atlanta would lose both its 1930 Union Station (demolished in 1971) and its downtown 1905 Terminal Station (razed in 1972). Its suburban Peachtree Station, now known as Brookwood Station, is today almost hopelessly inadequate for the needs of one of the South's largest and busiest cities.

The stations of Richmond, Virginia would suffer even more indignities at first. The city boasted no less than three grand passenger terminals. One of them was Broad Street Station, a domed neoclassical station built in 1919, that served the Richmond, Fredericksburg & Potomac and the Atlantic Coast Line railroads. Another was Main Street Station, built in 1901 and exemplifying French Renaissance style architecture, that served the Chesapeake & Ohio and Seaboard Air Line railroads. The third was compact Hull Street Station that served the Southern Railway. The latter two would lose their passenger train service before Amtrak took over, and Amtrak would forsake Broad Street Station in the mid-1970s for a stark, modern station to the northwest of town. Fortunately, all three survived. Hull Street Station was donated for use as a rail museum by a local rail enthusiast society chapter and Broad Street was converted to the Science Museum of Virginia in the 1980s. Main Street Station, after a series of fires and failed commercial developments that made the building appear jinxed, wound up in the hands of the Commonwealth of Virginia, which uses the building for offices and a restaurant.

Not every railroad completely forsook the passenger train in the mid-1900s. Several railroads continued to maintain and even rebuild passenger depots even in the face of declining traffic. The Norfolk & Western passenger station at Roanoke, built in 1904–5, was located in a major railroad headquarters, and had a railroad-owned, Tudor-style Hotel Roanoke adjacent to it. It was remodeled to a more contemporary style in 1947–49, and was reminiscent of more modern governmental office buildings or department stores, using a simple Art Deco combination of concrete and glass. The

ABOVE: The schedule board at the old Atchison, Topeka & Santa Fe RR's station at Trinidad, Colorado epitomizes the decline in passenger trains in the 1960s. From several transcontinental trains roaring past or stopping at the station daily, the station now sees but one pair of Amtrak trains a day, one in each direction.

< 55 >

< Train Stations >

ABOVE: By the 1950s, the changes to Pennsylvania Station, New York City, that were made over the decades had weakened the majesty of the original interior. Modern touches such as escalators and glass display cases are at odds against the classical interior that would soon fall to the wrecking ball.

rebuilding failed to stem the declining number of passengers, however, and only a token service lasted briefly beyond the formation of Amtrak (which decided to use a new economy terminal nearby).

The decline in passenger numbers was not the only cause of the decline of railroad stations. Freight traffic was on the decline and combined with the effects of consolidation, thousands of freight agents were out of a job, making their station offices redundant as well. Throughout the nation, secondary rail lines and freight-only branches were abandoned, leaving behind thousands of disused stations to fall to the elements.

In 1930, the major railroads of the United States operated 430,000 miles (691,999km) of trackage, but by 1980 they only operated 290,000 miles (466,697km). Wooden depots, built decades ago and already the victims of deferred maintenance, seldom stood a chance. A great majority of them were abandoned before the rail line was, and slowly decayed until demolished as a safety hazard. Many more were burned, sometimes to train firefighters, or were converted to feed or fertilizer warehouses.

The creation of Amtrak was not a salvation to many rural stations either, as might be imagined. Scores of stations that were barely surviving at stops throughout the truncated passenger network, still owned by the host railroads and not Amtrak, were boarded up or demolished. They were replaced by conductors selling tickets aboard the train and bus-stop-like shelters erected trackside with a simple schedule posted inside. Critics lambasted the shelters, calling them "Amshacks." Some Amtrak station stops, such as the one at Travis Road in San Antonio, Texas, in the early 1970s, didn't even earn the luxury of being a shelter. Especially insulting were the many shelters erected directly beside a surviving boarded-up station. Many of the stations that were replaced were eventually demolished as well.

The very first full station facility built by Amtrak, was erected in Cincinnati, Ohio, in 1972, specifically to bypass the majestic Cincinnati Union Terminal. The concourse over the tracks was demolished shortly thereafter, to make room for a piggyback freight terminal. The city purchased the remaining depot and leased it out for commercial development; the shopping mall that opened inside in 1980 failed soon after, a victim of declining neighborhood economics and a poor location.

Later efforts to provide more practical accommodations for passengers and service representatives led to a number of small, modern stations built by Amtrak or local agencies. These stations have served a variety of goals. Between Baltimore and Washington, the BWI Airport station serves a shuttle bus connecting directly to the Baltimore-Washington International Airport, and another at New Carrollton serves as a transfer point from commuter trains to the

< 56 >

< Chapter 4: Decay and Decline >

Washington Metro subway system. Both of these stations also offer easy highway access to the busy Northeast Corridor for suburbanites as well. At Hammond-Whiting, Indiana, a new station serves as both a local stop and a transfer point for passengers to change trains without having to enter Chicago's Union Station.

Even major city stations were not safe in the era of Amtrak and VIA Rail. By 1980, cutbacks mandated by reductions in government funding or low traffic levels saw the end of passenger service to the 1900-vintage Union Stations of Nashville, Tennessee and Louisville, Kentucky. It also saw the end to passenger trains at the 1901 Northern Pacific depot at Bismarck, North Dakota, and the 1906 NP station in Butte, Montana.

As late as 1996, Amtrak discontinued operating through Phoenix, Arizona and its 1923 Union Station. It was forced by its host railroad to operate on a more direct route and serve the city via a remote station to the south (now at Maricopa, site of the railroad car station previously mentioned). This move made Phoenix the largest city in North America without direct passenger train service. (Fortunately, all the vintage stations mentioned above survive intact today, converted to other uses.)

Of all the stations to fall to the wrecking ball, however, none was a greater loss than New York City's Pennsylvania Station. By the 1950s, the majestic 1910 terminal was tired, dirty, and had had its original grandeur altered by gradual interior reconstruction. In October 1963, the financially ailing Pennsylvania Railroad sold the air rights over its station to developers, and demolition began in earnest shortly thereafter, lasting for two years. Legal challenges and protests were to no avail. The rail facilities were replaced by a claustrophobic underground concourse indistinguishable in spirit from a subway station.

In place of the Roman-style temple rose Madison Square Garden, a metal and glass sports arena. The rubble from the old station was ignominiously dumped into the swamps of the Meadowlands in New Jersey. The effect upon the people of New York was comparable to discovering the Statue of Liberty replaced by a glass office tower, or Parisians suddenly finding the Eiffel Tower replaced by a roller coaster.   <

BELOW: The Southern Pacific RR's wooden depot at Lone Pine, California was built as part of the Southern Pacific's "Jawbone" line from Mojave to Owenyo. It was completed in 1910 to haul construction supplies for the Los Angeles Aqueduct and connect with the Southern Pacific's narrow-gauge lines to the north into Nevada. The line was abandoned around 1980. The depot has since been renovated and restored as a private residence.

< 59 >

< Train Stations >

< 58 >

Chapter 5
Reuse, Restore, Revival

> If railroading in the public eye was to go into a decline during the later part of the 20th century, it also appeared that a great many railroad stations were not allowed to follow suit. Although the majority of depots are now but a memory, the survivors have been entrusted with keeping the memories alive. It is estimated that over 10,000 railroad stations in North America survive in some form, the majority as a result of preservation.

The demolition of Pennsylvania Station in New York has been credited with doing more to galvanize the historic preservation movement and protect other historic structures nationwide than any other action in the 20th century. In the wake of the demolition, the New York City Landmarks Preservation Commission found the political wherewithal to back its words with actions and legislation. On a national level, the U.S. Congress passed the National Historic Preservation Act (NHPA) in October 1966. The NHPA would expand the options for increasing the number of structures on the National Register of Historic Places; a national inventory of sites deemed of historical and/or cultural importance. A variety of options to nurture preservation efforts were passed in the following years. These were in the form of tax incentives for private enterprise, and grants to identify and preserve historic structures. Perhaps most important among these was the Intermodal Surface Transportation Efficiency Act of 1991, which designated $155 billion in funds over six years for transportation projects. This included $3 billion in "enhancement funds," which could be used to restore facilities along historic transportation corridors. The popular program was extended and expanded with the passage of the Transportation Equity Act for the 21st Century (TEA-21) in June 1998.

The loss of a huge landmark, such as Pennsylvania Station, along with the losses of other stations large and small throughout America, called attention to the position of railroad stations as cultural icons. It also indirectly spurred innumerable local, small-scale, and large-scale preservation projects, as well as making the demolition of more of the great city stations a far more difficult mission.

TOP LEFT: The Riverside, Pennsylvania, depot, an ex-Pennsylvania RR station, represents a sterling example of a commercial restoration of a station, in this case into a gift shop. Seen here in 1989 with Christmas lights twinkling and a Delaware & Hudson freight with a New York, Susquehanna & Western B40-8 locomotive, the station has since been vacated, but survives today.

BOTTOM LEFT: When excursion operations started over the Belfast & Moosehead Lake Railroad in central Maine in the late 1980s, the railroad—now owned by the city of Belfast—rehabilitated its Unity, Maine combination depot to serve passengers for the first time since it ended regular passenger traffic in 1960. The station now houses the excursion railroad standard combination of ticket office and gift shop.

< 59 >

< Train Stations >

ABOVE: The Barber Junction, North Carolina, was built in 1898 at the junction of two Southern Railway lines between Charlotte and Winston-Salem, and between Salisbury and Asheville. Abandoned at the end of passenger service in 1968, it was relocated in 1980 to the nearby North Carolina Transportation Museum at Spencer. Repainted in the Southern's 1925 standard paint scheme of green with yellow trim, the building features segregated waiting rooms, common in the South at the time of construction.

RIGHT: The Beverly Shores depot, Indiana, of the Chicago South Shore & South Bend RR was built in 1929 near the dunes of Lake Michigan. It combines the Mediterranean revival styling of stucco and red barrel tiles (matching many houses in town built at the same time) with Art Deco neon signage. It included a five-room residence for the station agent. Recently restored, the commuter railroad still stops at the station.

Much assistance for these efforts came from the National Trust for Historic Preservation, a quasi-public agency organized in 1949, which has often highlighted railroad stations and even entire railroads for preservation action.

One of the primary goals of these preservation movements was to reverse the trend of railroads abandoning major terminals, and make the terminals once again a viable destination in their own right. This process was often long and arduous. By this point in its history, the typical terminal was often a dingy, dirty shell, horrendously underutilized and unattractive to commercial enterprise, much like the downtown areas that often surrounded them. Through the use of various incentives, such as those described above, cities targeted both the terminal depots and the surrounding areas for redevelopment, combining both public and private investment. The results breathed new life into many a classic station.

Washington Union Terminal, a flagship station on Amtrak's Northeast Corridor and a next-door neighbor to the United States Capitol, was the site of one of the most spectacular and successful projects. The station languished for years after a failed attempt to construct a visitors' center, before Amtrak invested $70 million into the colossal property to repair the building, and restore architectural details. This was soon followed by $50 million in private development funds to tastefully convert much of the wrecked interior to multilevel retail and commercial space. $40 million was spent in city funds to construct a parking garage above the tracks to the rear. The revived station reopened in 1988, and the joint investment has resulted in a combined retail, dining, and transportation

< 60 >

< Chapter 5: Reuse, Restore, Revival >

center that has been successful beyond expectations, bringing life and vibrancy to a landmark of the nation's capital.

In St. Louis, another similar retail rehabilitation began not long after Amtrak quit the station for smaller quarters. Funded by federal grant money, tax credits, and private investment, the station was restored and rebuilt, and reopened in 1985. The shed is filled with shops and restaurants, and the headhouse features a six-story hotel, incorporating a variety of the structure's inner areas, including the old Terminal Hotel.

In Cincinnati, after partial demolition and the failure of a shopping mall tenant—a series of fits and starts not uncommon to such projects—a complete rehabilitation of the abandoned Cincinnati Union Terminal began in 1984 and lasted until 1990. In 1991 the Amtrak service was restored and the cathedral of Art Deco now houses a pair of history museums, and a movie theater.

Cities far outside the reach of passenger train travel have also rescued their cities' downtown terminals. The city of Scranton, Pennsylvania, lost its last passenger service in the mid-1960s. The vast, six-story Delaware, Lackawanna & Western passenger depot, built in 1908 in the French Renaissance style, was left as a mostly empty office building; a state of affairs that could not continue, because the building occupied the downtown district like a giant cornerstone. In the early 1980s, local political leaders lobbied to relocate the Steamtown Foundation, a private railroad museum collection, from Vermont to disused railroad facilities in Scranton, and declare it a National Historic Site. Concurrently, a developer was brought in to rehabilitate the depot into a luxury hotel in 1983. The rehabilitation brought back the spectacular interior, with a skylighted ceiling and a huge open lobby with interior balconies. In 2001 a similar hotel renovation with 72 rooms was proposed for the smaller, 1911 Pennsylvania Station in Baltimore, Maryland. This station, however, remains as a very active Amtrak Northeast Corridor and Maryland Rail Commuter station as well.

The number of major city depots is tiny, however, compared to the small-town depots scattered widely across America. Like their larger brethren, they too suffered as the railroads retreated from

ABOVE: The Ogden (Utah) Union Depot, built to an Italian Renaissance Revival style in 1924 to replace an earlier depot that burned, served the Union Pacific, Southern Pacific, and Denver & Rio Grande Western Railroads. In the later days of private passenger train operations by the railroads, the tracks behind Ogden became the site where cars from multiple trains were, in the words of one writer, "shuffled like a deck of canasta cards" before resuming their respective journeys. The station buildings were donated to the city after the coming of Amtrak, and now house museums, a restaurant, a theater, meeting rooms, civic offices, and railroad offices.

< 61 >

< Chapter 5: Reuse, Restore, Revival >

American life. Many were simply boarded up after closure, usually after years of neglect by the railroad, before they were abandoned.

Long before the preservation movement took hold in the United States, abandoned stations were purchased for reuse by private individuals. The basic design of many combination stations, however, made adaptation to a dwelling somewhat challenging. Large rooms, open rafters, and high ceilings made heating and cooling the property a lot more difficult. Nonetheless, many a disused station became a private residence, a retail store or office, a lumberyard, farm supply office, or even a shed. Many such structures were moved to new locations, but others could not be moved because there were no tracks left to move them. A rare few were permitted to reside or operate businesses in stations beside active freight tracks. Additions to the original structure, to facilitate extra rooms not found in an original station, such as a bathroom or a kitchen, often disguised the original architecture of the depot.

One extremely popular reuse for railroad stations across North America is as a restaurant. The open spaces and fine architecture typical in so many stations almost beg for use as a restaurant dining area. The agent's office often serves as a bar area, and former waiting rooms are used as kitchens or are located in new additions to the building. Such additions are often necessary to retain the historic integrity of a station that may be owned by a preservation-minded municipality or agency. The restaurants installed are often outfitted with railroad-theme décor and historic photographs or items of railroadiana. The reuse of a station as a restaurant or tavern has become such a cliché in North America that one noted rail writer has expressed that his greatest fantasy in railroading was to purchase a restaurant and convert it into a railroad station.

Many of the more ambitious restaurateurs acquired retired rail passenger cars, installed them adjacent to their station, and incorporated the rebuilt cars as additional "authentic" dining areas. Seldom were the cars actual dining cars, but it mattered little to generations of patrons, who may well never have taken a passenger train in their lives, let alone been served a meal in a moving train. A visitor to the 1910 ex-Pennsylvania RR Front Street Station restaurant in Northumberland, Pennsylvania, will find that two former Delaware, Lackawanna & Western (DL&W)

LEFT: The B&O's Point of Rocks Station, Maryland, was designed by E. Francis Baldwin and represents a fantastic example of the Gothic Revival style. Built in 1873–75 on a triangle between two main tracks (the B&O lines to Baltimore and Washington, D.C.) and a connecting track (behind the station), it survives today as a Maryland Rail Commuter train stop.

BELOW: The former Southern Pacific depot in San Antonio, Texas (built in 1903 by the Galveston, Harrisburg & San Antonio) continues to be used as a passenger train stop today. The so-called Spanish Renaissance style depot was restored in the 1980s to its 1940s appearance.

< 65 >

< Train Stations >

RIGHT: *The distinctive and unique depot at North Conway, New Hampshire, built by the Portsmouth, Great Falls & Conway RR in 1874, was designed by Nathaniel J. Bradlee, who also later designed the Union Station in Portland, Maine in 1888. Closed in the early 1960s by the Boston & Maine RR, the unique station is now preserved by the Conway Scenic RR and used as its main depot for its steam and diesel excursion trains.*

BELOW: *An original sign on the restored East Broad Top RR station and headquarters in Orbisonia, Pennsylvania.*

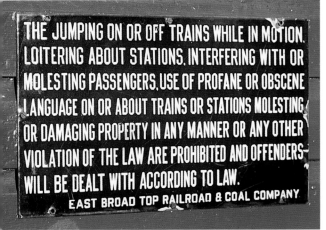

THE JUMPING ON OR OFF TRAINS WHILE IN MOTION. LOITERING ABOUT STATIONS. INTERFERING WITH OR MOLESTING PASSENGERS, USE OF PROFANE OR OBSCENE LANGUAGE ON OR ABOUT TRAINS OR STATIONS MOLESTING OR DAMAGING PROPERTY IN ANY MANNER OR ANY OTHER VIOLATION OF THE LAW ARE PROHIBITED AND OFFENDERS WILL BE DEALT WITH ACCORDING TO LAW.
EAST BROAD TOP RAILROAD & COAL COMPANY

cars serve as part of the banquet hall, itself added to the station's southern end. Diners can be entertained, or distracted, by the passing of freight trains on the adjacent main line and interchange track. The hometown short-line railroad has its offices nearby in a former DL&W freight house itself. Sadly, unless they are kept under a separate roof, railroad cars present difficult challenges for maintenance and weatherproofing. A number of former railroad car eateries have been scuttled or scrapped, and often rail preservationists or museums have claimed parts from the unrestorable cars to use on preserved equipment instead.

A few other larger stations in the United States were converted into brewery restaurants, known as "brewpubs," during the craft-beer revival of the 1980s and 1990s. Most even carried on the railroad theme to the naming of their beers and the restaurant's décor. A notable example is the Titletown Restaurant & Brewery in the former Chicago & North Western (C&NW) station in downtown Green Bay, Wisconsin. The depot was designed by principal C&NW architect Charles Frost and built in 1899 on a former freight yard site that used to be across the river from Green Bay. It features a Venetian design with a tall campanile tower with four clock faces on the street side, balanced below by the long trackside platform and sheds. Railroads used the depot as office space until 1994, and the building was later purchased by investors and renovated. The brewery was built inside and opened in December 1996. A return of passenger service to the city has not been ruled out, and if it occurs a portion of the depot will most assuredly be used.

The Flossmoor Station Brewery in the Illinois Central depot in Flossmoor, Illinois has commuter trains to and from Chicago stopping outside, and has acquired a former IC caboose for display and party space outside the station on a short stretch of track. The Red Star Brewery and Restaurant in the 1911 Pennsylvania RR station in Greensburg, Pennsylvania, shares its building with a business office, and also serves as an unmanned Amtrak stop. The Embudo Station Restaurant & Brewery in Embudo, New Mexico resides in a former Denver & Rio Grande Western station that lost its railroad line in the 1940s. It also hosts a river rafting business as a sideline. In 1998 the Railyard Pub and South Shore Brewery was founded in the stone Soo Lone depot in Ashland, Wisconsin, built in 1889. Tragically, the station was struck by fire in April 2000, and the brewery was forced to relocate elsewhere while restoration of the building was undertaken by city officials. Another "station brewery" of sorts was opened in Aurora, Illinois. The Chicago, Burlington & Quincy stone "roundhouse," which was one of the oldest locomotive servicing facilities built in the 1850s, was converted into two facilities. It

< 64 >

< Train Stations >

ABOVE: *The 1910 Atchison, Topeka & Santa Fe (AT&SF) depot in Amarillo, Texas was constructed in a Spanish Colonial Revival style, popular on the AT&SF system. It featured waiting rooms segregated by both gender and race, as well as a Harvey House restaurant. Passenger traffic ceased in 1971 with the coming of Amtrak, and the depot has seen unsuccessful commercial development.*

became both the Aurora Transportation Facility, an intermodal station replacing an earlier station up the line, and the America's Brewpub restaurant.

As railroads reduced their operations in more urban areas, an enlightened awareness of the role railroad stations play as local icons aroused efforts across the nation to preserve and to maintain a civic function for the structure in some capacity. Many preserved stations have been rebuilt into city halls, police stations, court offices, tourist promotion centers, bus depots, public meeting places, or even a fire station, as was the case in Wallingford, Vermont, for a time. Many rail stations, which have a passenger train service, albeit at a reduced rate from the heyday of railroading, have been adapted into "intermodal" stations. They often serve rail passengers, intercity bus lines, and city bus transit lines. The 1887 Pennsylvania RR station in Harrisburg, Pennsylvania, complete with vintage trainsheds still in use, is a remarkable example of such a project. In many other cases, a station building is acquired and owned by the municipality, the county, or a civil agency, which reasonably guarantees the building's survival. The building is then leased out to an appropriate tenant for reuse as an office or other business. Unfortunately, in a great many instances stations preserved by well-intentioned civil servants have often been vacant after their rescue and renovation. Such preservation often appears to follow a policy of "save it now, and we'll figure out what to do with it later."

One notable example of this syndrome is one of the oldest city station structures standing in America—the Baltimore & Ohio Camden Station in Baltimore, Maryland, that opened in 1856 and was completed in 1865. The historic brick building, a rich mixture of Italianate, Greek Revival, and Georgian architecture, was by the 1980s a run-down vacant structure. It served morning and evening

< 66 >

< Chapter 5: Reuse, Restore, Revival >

commuter trains to and from Washington D.C. The ticketing and waiting room functions were even replaced for a time by an old railroad passenger car, a tactic unheard of in the 1980s. From 1990–92 the popular Oriole Park at Camden Yards baseball stadium was developed on former railroad property adjacent to it. It was purchased by the Maryland Stadium Authority to restore the original Camden Station to a semblance of its former appearance. Yet except for a brief exhibition, it has remained vacant and locked ever since. None of its proposed uses, such as an office, or a baseball museum, have come to fruition. A newer building with platforms, serving both commuter trains and light rail tracks, replaced the railroad car, which was donated to the nearby B&O Railroad Museum.

Efforts at station preservation are never a guarantee for the future. Wooden stations are vulnerable to the ravages of arson, rot, and inadequate maintenance. In 1993 a pre-Civil War station in Petersburg, Virginia, was destroyed by a tornado, and in 1992 the Florida East Coast depot from Princeton, Florida, that was moved to the Gold Coast Railroad Museum in Miami, was completely obliterated by a hurricane. Several other stations over the years, including the 1872 brick Pennsylvania RR passenger station in Sunbury, Pennsylvania, and the 1902 stone Grand Trunk Western depot in Lansing, Michigan, have been seriously damaged or destroyed by derailing trains or trucks struck by trains at road crossings. Both stations were rebuilt, and survive today.

One of the most popular civic reuses for a station is as a local museum, which is seen as a perfect use for a structure with its own history. In a vast majority of cases, the museum is at least partially dedicated to the history of railroading. However, there are a great

BELOW: The Grand Trunk RR (later the Grand Trunk Western RR) built this spectacular Jacobean Revival depot in Lansing, Michigan in 1902, spurning the Union Depot built in the same year by the Michigan Central and Pere Marquette RRs. It was converted to a restaurant in the early 1970s, and continues in this role today.

< 61 >

many railroad stations that have been targeted for preservation specifically as railroad museums. Civic organizations and railroad enthusiast groups, such as local chapters of the National Railway Historical Society, have preserved stations as railroad museums. They appear in such diverse places as: Greenport, New York (Long Island RR); Dennison, Ohio (Pennsylvania RR); Cowan, Tennessee (Nashville, Chattanooga & St. Louis RR); Goleta, California (Southern Pacific RR); Rossville, Illinois (Chicago & Eastern Illinois RR); Hamlet, N.C. (Seaboard Air Line); and Temple, Texas (Missouri, Kansas & Texas RR; an Atchison, Topeka & Santa Fe RR station was moved to the site from Moody, Texas, in 1973).

A station does not have to be a 19th-century relic to be a target for preservationists. Recent efforts have saved the 1940s Mendota, Illinois, depot and converted it into a museum. A rail photography museum is planned for the Norfolk & Western passenger station in Roanoke, Virginia, which was purchased in 2000 by the Western Virginia Foundation for the Arts and Sciences for that purpose.

Some railroad stations, such as the ones in Council Bluffs, Iowa (Chicago, Rock Island & Pacific RR), Severna Park, Maryland, (Baltimore & Annapolis interurban), Vienna, Virginia, (Washington & Old Dominion RR) and Clovis, New Mexico (Atchison, Topeka & Santa Fe RR) house model railroad clubs, which construct miniature model railroad layouts inside. Other railroad depot museums have incorporated a model railroad as part of their display as well.

Perhaps one of the most ambitious private projects has been undertaken by the Pennsylvania Railroad Technical & Historical Society. In the 1990s they acquired the 1849 vintage brick Pennsylvania RR station at Lewistown Junction, Pennsylvania, restoring it to more closely approximate its original appearance. They also renovated it to house an ever-expanding archive of artifacts, documents, and photographs from the archives of, or relating to, the Pennsylvania RR. Not only did they recreate a hometown environment, but they advanced the preservation of railroad information that spans many states.

A similar project was undertaken by the Maryland & Pennsylvania RR Preservation Society. In 1992 they acquired not only eight abandoned miles (13km) of the namesake railroad's right of way, but the entire village of Muddy Creek Forks, Pennsylvania, including the 1900 A.M. Grove general store and station, and the adjacent roller mill. The properties are now owned by a county authority, and the society manages the properties. The station-store has been restored as a general store and station museum, and efforts continue on the track and mill.

Railroad station museums, of course, need not be dedicated exclusively to railroad history. Often, the station's museum is dedicated to local history in general. The joint Southern Ry.–Blue Ridge

LEFT: The Denver & Rio Grande Western combination depot in Chama, New Mexico, built in 1899 to replace an earlier depot that burned down, serves a surviving section of the once-extensive Colorado narrow-gauge railroad network. Part of a rich "time capsule" of original, intact steam railroad facilities, the station now serves as offices for the state-owned Cumbres & Toltec Scenic RR.

< Train Stations >

ABOVE: The 1905, brick Pennsylvania RR depot at Perryville, Maryland, was built in the middle of a triangle formed by the junction of a major freight line connecting to a busy passenger route. Built to a Colonial Revival style, it was refurbished in the early 1990s to serve a restored commuter rail service to Baltimore and Washington. It also houses a small railroad museum.

Railway depot in Belton, South Carolina, built in 1910, houses two separate museums. These are the Ruth Drake Museum, dedicated to early life in Belton and Anderson Counties, and the South Carolina Tennis Hall of Fame.

Many other stations are owned by, and used as museums for, the local town or county historical society. Among these are the neatly trimmed Victorian depot in Potter Place, New Hampshire, (Boston & Maine, 1874); the brick 1902 Chicago & North Western depot at Sleepy Eye, Minnesota; and the 1910 Sumpter Valley Railway, two-story, wooden depot in Prairie City, Oregon.

In many instances, railroads have been willing to donate or make available stations along active railroads with the provision that the structure be moved away from railroad property. In the case of a small wooden structure, such a move is not difficult. Many of these depots are simply moved back a short distance from the track, as was done with the Pennsylvania RR depot in La Plata, Maryland, for a local history museum. Or they are moved to a local park or museum space, as was done with two tiny depots in Cape May County, New Jersey, which were relocated to a "village" of historic structures. Such a move can prove difficult in the case of a brick or stone station, but not impossible. This was proved in the 1990s by the two-block relocation of the stone 1902 Cleveland, Cincinnati, Chicago & St. Louis station in Lafayette, Indiana. The station was reconfigured to serve as an upgraded Amtrak and bus station, and has an original floor at street level and a new floor at track level.

The Lafayette station project also represents an example of perhaps the greatest thrill and goal for station preservationists—restoring a station to its original intended purpose as a railroad service,

< 70 >

< Chapter 5: Reuse, Restore, Revival >

while preserving it for the future. This can be done in a variety of ways. Amtrak, VIA Rail, or commuter service can be restored to a rail line or re-routed to a different line, necessitating the use of at least part of a station as a waiting room and/or ticket office. Occasionally, waiting rooms or ticket offices that were previously closed for a long time will be re-opened to serve passengers, as was done with the Pennsylvania RR Lewistown Junction station mentioned earlier. Many small commuter stations, now owned by local transit agencies, have been partially leased to small businesses catering to commuter needs. This could be in the form of coffee shops, newsstands, and dry-cleaning shops.

In an amazing bit of irony, Amtrak has occasionally not been able to gain access to a former passenger station for passenger use. In some cases, logistical problems such as track layout have made such access problematic. In another case in Montgomery, Alabama, no space was available at the handsomely restored and commercially redeveloped Victorian Gothic, Romanesque-style Union Station, built in 1898. Amtrak had to create a station in the base of a concrete grain elevator on the other side of the tracks.

Another savior of old terminals has sprung up with the recent revival of commuter trains in many regions. In response to increasing highway congestion, many metropolitan areas have started to think about passenger trains, in the form of either conventional locomotive-hauled trains or self-propelled light-rail cars. Railroad commuter service has been established, or re-established, in places such as northern Virginia, Dallas, Miami, Seattle-Tacoma, and even car-crazy Los Angeles and remote Northern Vermont. Unfortunately, however, the modern model of commuter operations

ABOVE: The majestic brick passenger station at Lansdale, Pennsylvania, was built in 1902–4. It replaced a wooden 1868 structure, and is today used by SEPTA (Southeastern Pennsylvania Transportation Author-ity) commuter trains.

BELOW: The "yin-yang" logo of the Northern Pacific Railroad was incorporated into this mosaic decorating the wall of the 1901 depot in Missoula, Montana.

< 71 >

< Train Stations >

ABOVE & FAR RIGHT: Built in 1908, the International & Great Northern (later Missouri Pacific RR) depot in San Antonio, Texas, features a stained-glass rose window incorporating the railroad's logo. Closed by the railroad in 1970, the depot languished for years before it was purchased by a local credit union for office use. The eight-foot-high statue of an Indian shooting an arrow towards Fort Sam Houston was stolen during the station's abandonment, but surreptitiously returned during restoration.

BELOW RIGHT: In 1890, the Philadelphia & Reading RR (later Reading RR) built this combination depot at Rushland, Pennsylvania, when the line was extended to New Hope. The line is now part of the New Hope & Ivyland tourist railroad, although the station is not a regular stop on its excursion service.

involves stripped-down, highly automated operations with small shelters and automated ticket machines. Although some vintage stations have been refurbished, and many new ones built, the realistic prognosis for station preservation for new commuter operations is not great. Three very notable exceptions to the rule, however, are located along the Caltrain commuter line between San Francisco and San Jose, California.

Santa Clara boasts what is believed to be the oldest surviving depot in the United States west of the Mississippi River, parts of it dating to 1863. The original wooden station was built to the standard plans of San Francisco & San Jose, who were the predecessors of Southern Pacific RR, to serve Santa Clara college and local farms. It was moved across the tracks and expanded in 1877. The state purchased it to use for its commuter trains in the 1980s, and it was rehabilitated to shelter a historical society museum in the old freight and baggage section, while serving passengers in the oldest section.

In Menlo Park, the San Francisco & San Jose RR built the original wooden depot in 1867 to serve a growing community. It was expanded over the years, and Victorian gingerbread detailing, such as ridgetop cresting, patterned shingles, the agent's bay window, and bargeboards, were added in the late 1890s. The station was acquired by the state in 1987 and restored to its 1917 appearance, but was later restyled to match local tastes after some criticism.

The substantially larger 1894 Burlingame depot was among the first depots to be built in the Spanish Mission style. This was a style that gained a great deal of popularity in station design throughout the Southwestern states on the Santa Fe and Southern Pacific lines.

< 72 >

< Train Stations >

ABOVE: Although portions of the combination depot reportedly date back to the 1860s, the former Northern Central (later PRR) combination depot has been restored to a more accurate 1935 appearance. Formerly serving the junction of the PRR and the Stewartstown RR, it is now being refurbished as a museum, community center, and visitors' center for the York County Rail Heritage Trail.

The design work was executed by architects J.B. Mathisen and George H. Howard Jr., who not coincidentally were members of the Burlingame Country Club that had lobbied for the station in the first place. Residential development around the station, of course, was another goal of the club members, and it worked. With simulated adobe construction, the roof even included authentic handmade roofing tiles salvaged from derelict missions. From 1983, local residents lobbied for restoration of the decaying station. This began in 1984 and finished in 1986, including repainting the station to its original mustard-yellow color.

Often, a tourist excursion operation that uses vintage steam or diesel locomotives and passenger stock, will begin operation over a little-used or abandoned railroad. It will utilize an existing depot or relocate an existing structure to serve as the line's station. One of America's most famous tourist railroads, the Strasburg RR in Pennsylvania, disassembled the wooden 1880s Reading RR depot at East Petersburg into nine sections. They hauled it 20 miles, and reassembled it at their new terminus east of Strasburg, Pennsylvania, soon after its excursion operations began in 1959. The Wilmington & Western RR in Delaware moved not one, but two stations to its Greenbank terminal area in 1965. One was an original 1872 station from Yorklyn, Delaware, also on the branch on which it operated, and the other a small Pennsylvania RR station from Kennedyville, Maryland. As with a great many tourist operations, the line has outgrown its historic structures, and has recently constructed a new building to fully serve customers. The Yorklyn depot has been relegated to house a museum and the Kennedyville structure has been moved to the other end of its line.

The Mid-Continent Railway Museum began looking for a station for its facility shortly after moving to a site near New Freedom,

< 76 >

< Chapter 5: Reuse, Restore, Revival >

Wisconsin in 1963. It had the chance to acquire the downtown Chicago & North Western RR depot, but chose instead to relocate the attractive Chicago & North Western wooden depot from nearby Rock Springs instead. The station, formerly known as Ablemans, was built in 1894. It was moved to the museum site in December 1965, and was restored originally as the museum's gift shop and ticket office. Fire damaged the structure in 1970, and the ensuing rebuilding included a more accurate restoration job, complete with authentic paint schemes.

Many other excursion lines have incorporated the line's original stations into their operations. Another Pennsylvania tourist line, the New Hope and Ivyland RR, reclaimed the town's original wooden depot with its "witch's hat" roof, which had been moved out of town to serve as a hunting lodge in the 1950s, and relocated it close to its original location in the 1960s. Another original station with a conical tower was restored in the 1970s, and is in use by another rail excursion operation. This one is a brick structure built by the Central RR of New Jersey in Jim Thorpe, originally named Mauch Chunk, Pennsylvania, in 1888.

The Conway Scenic Railroad in New Hampshire was founded in 1974 on a rail line with one of the nation's most colorful, distinctive and beautiful stations. North Conway's wooden depot incorporates both Victorian and Czarist Russian architecture, and was built by Boston & Maine's predecessor Portsmouth, Great Falls & Conway RR in 1874. Locals purchased the station initially for preservation in 1963, but the efforts to buy or lease the rail line for continued railroad operation lasted for over a decade after that.

The narrow-gauge East Broad Top RR in Pennsylvania still uses its original 1906 office building and station in the twin towns of Orbisonia and Rockhill Furnace. The station is part of a privately owned operation that runs short excursion trains behind original steam locomotives. The entire complex, including locomotives, cars, shop buildings, roundhouse, station, and railroad, are original and complete from the day the 35-mile (56km) freight railroad ceased operation in 1956. It existed for the most part like an insect preserved in amber, unaltered save for the ravages of nature and the excursion operation. Deferred maintenance,

BELOW: The original Philadelphia & Reading station at Bryn Athyn, Pennsylvania, on a branch to Newtown was simply space leased out of a local building. In 1902, the railroad erected a new combination depot on land donated by a local property association. Passenger commuter service on the line ended in 1983, and the quaint depot now serves as the local post office.

< 75 >

< Train Stations >

ABOVE: *Part of the historic value of the East Broad Top narrow gauge railroad in Orbisonia, Pennsylvania, is the ability to create "time-capsule" scenes and moments like this. A recreation of an early morning scene shows baggage waiting for a train of almost a hundred years earlier, complete with original carts and signs at the authentic 1906 depot and headquarters building.*

however, has led the National Trust for Historic Preservation to nominate the entire railroad as one of the nation's most endangered historic sites. An unaffilliated East Broad Top RR enthusiast group has acquired the railroad's Robertsdale depot, two valleys and two tunnels away from Orbisonia, for preservation. A third depot between the two in Saltillo survives only by the grace of the termites holding hands.

The Grand Canyon RR in Arizona, which re-established passenger train travel to the Grand Canyon over the Santa Fe's defunct branch line in 1989, operates out of two original depots. The northern end terminates yards from the canyon rim at the Atchison Topeka & Santa Fe's 1910 Ponderosa log depot, now owned by the National Park Service. Forty miles to the south at the former junction is the Santa Fe's Williams Depot and Fray Marcos Hotel, built in Italian Renaissance style from reinforced concrete in 1908, and now used as offices and station facilities by the excursion line.

Other excursion railroad operations using the line's original depots include the Yreka Western RR in California, which uses the 1910 Yreka RR depot in its namesake town, and the Durango & Silverton RR in Durango, Colorado, which uses the 1881 Denver & Rio Grande RR depot. A few rare railroads manage to use the original stations as headquarters for both a passenger excursion operation and a co-existing freight railroad operation. Among these are the California Western RR's station in Fort Bragg, California, and the Arcade & Attica RR's station in Arcade, New York, which was

< 76 >

< Chapter 5: Reuse, Restore, Revival >

originally a house before being purchased by the railroad and converted in 1900.

Even the lack of a railroad track does not preclude a station's use for tourist transportation needs. As of 2001, over 11,000 miles (17,700km) of abandoned railroad rights of way have been preserved, minus the tracks, or beside unused or little-used ones, as pedestrian, bicycle, and equestrian trails. Proposals are in place for up to 20,000 more miles to be used in this way. Federal laws passed in 1983 permit the preservation of a rail corridor intact, in a process called "rail banking" for potential future use for other modes of transit. These could include electric light rail, subway, or reinstalled freight lines in the future and pedestrian uses in the interim. Stations in places such as Monkton, Maryland, (once Pennsylvania RR, now Northern Central Trail), White Top, Virginia, (once Norfolk & Western, now Virginia Creeper Trail), and Garnett, Kansas, (once Atchison, Topeka & Santa Fe, now Prairie Spirit Rail-Trail), have been adapted for use as visitor centers, ranger stations, and rest stops along adjacent rail trails.

Railroad stations have even spawned their own special interest society, the Railroad Station Historical Society, Inc. It was formed in the fall of 1967, loosely organized around a number of Great Plains depot enthusiasts that realized depots were fast disappearing from trackside. The society unites those with a common interest in not only stations, but other railroad structures such as signal towers, engine houses, coaling and water towers, and even bridges and tunnels. Members have advanced the study of stations and other structures by photographing and collecting data, writing articles and histories, and collecting vintage postcards, a surprisingly valuable resource for information on lesser stations. More recently, members and affiliates have been constructing numerous Internet websites, complete with databases listing surviving stations, and often extinct ones, and offer vintage and modern images. The society maintains an archive, publishes a bi-monthly publication and has its own website (www.rrshs.org).

Another advocacy foundation, The Great American Station Foundation, was created in 1996 to "revitalize communities through new construction or conversion and restoration of existing rail passenger stations, and the possible conversion of historic non-railroad structures to active station use." As the organization has grown and evolved, it has set its goal to become the national intermediary organization not only for station revitalization, but also for community revitalization in areas surrounding intercity, commuter and urban rail stations. The nonprofit agency maintains a staff to work for the preservation and conversion of stations through existing grant programs and monies, and also offers a web site for those wishing to learn more on the subject (www.stationfoundation.org).<

< 77 >

Bibliography

> Several hundred books on railroad stations, depots, and terminals have been written in North America. They cover everything from the history of an individual small-town station to stations of a particular railroad to an attempt to cover every aspect of station history. A great many are specialized far beyond the focus of the general reader or historian.

The following general interest books are believed to be of the most use to the reader of this book wishing to find out more about stations. Although many are out of print, copies may surface at better libraries or used bookstores. Particularly recommended is Janet Greenstein Potter's *Great American Railroad Stations*, a state-by-state guidebook to many of the most notable preserved depots.

Alexander, Edwin P, *Down at the Depot American Railroad Stations from 1831 to 1920*. New York: Bramhall House, 1970.

Anderson Notter Finegold, Inc, *Recycling Historic Railroad Stations; A Citizen's Manual*. Washington, DC: U.S. Department of Transportation, 1978.

Anon, *Back on Track: A Guide to New Uses for Old Depots*. Little Rock, AR: Arkansas Historic Preservation Program, 1993.

Berg, Walter E, *Buildings and Structures of American Railroads*. New York: John Wiley & Sons, 1893 (Reprinted 1977, Newton K. Gregg).

Bye, Randolph, *The Vanishing Depot*. Wynnewood, PA: Livingston Publishing, 1973.

Cavalier, Julian, *North American Railroad Stations*. Cranbury, NJ: A.S. Barnes, 1979.

Cavalier, Julian, *Classic American Railroad Stations*. San Diego, CA: A.S. Barnes, 1980.

Douglas, Gordon H, *All Aboard! The Railroad in American Life*. New York: Marlowe & Co., 1994.

Droege, John A, *Passenger Terminals and Trains*. New York: McGraw-Hill, 1916, Reprinted 1969, Kalmbach Publishing.

Edmonson, Harold A and Richard V Francaviglia (eds.), *Railroad Station Planbook*. Milwaukee, WI: Kalmbach Publishing, 1977.

Empire State Railway Museum, *Guide to Tourist Railroads and Museums*. Waukesha, WI: Kalmbach Publishing, published annually.

< 78 >

< Bibliography >

Grant, H Roger, *Living in the Depot: The Two-Story Railroad Station*. Iowa City, IA: University of Iowa Press, 1993.

Grant, H Roger and Bohi, Charles W, *The Country Railroad Station in America*. Boulder, CO: Pruett Publishing, 1978. Revised ed. Sioux Falls, SD: Center for Western Studies, 1988.

Grow, Lawrence, *Waiting for the 5:05: Terminal, Station, and Depot in America*. New York: Main Street/Universe Books, 1977.

Grow, Lawrence, *On the 8:02: An Informal History of Commuting by Rail in America*. New York: Mayflower Books, 1979.

Halberstadt, Hans and Halberstadt, April, *Great American Train Stations Classic Terminals and Depots*. New York: Barnes & Noble Books, 1997 (Originally published as *The American Train Depot and Roundhouse*. Osceola, WI: Motorbooks International, 1996).

Huls, Mary E, *Adaptive Reuse of Railroad Stations*. Monticello, IL: Vance Bibliographies, 1986.

Lewis, Edward A, *New England Country Depots*. Arcade, New York: The Baggage Car, 1973.

Martin, J Edward, *Railway Stations of Western Canada: An Architectural History*. White Rock, BC: Studio E Martin, 1980.

Meeks, Carroll LV, *The Railroad Station: An Architectural History*. New Haven, CT: Yale University Press, 1956.

Potter, Janet Greenstein, *Great American Railroad Stations*. New York: John Wiley & Sons, 1996.

Richards, Jeffrey and Mackenzie, John M, *The Railway Station: A Social History*. Oxford, England: Oxford University Press, 1986.

Rutherford, Scott, *Classic American Railroad Terminals*. Motorbooks, 2000.

Seto, JW, *Railroad Stations in the U.S.* Chicago, IL: Council of Planning Librarians, 1978.

Traser, Donald R, *Virginia Railway Depots*. Richmond, VA: Old Dominion Chapter National Railway Historical Society, 1999.

Van Trump, James D, *Railroad Stations of Pennsylvania*. Glenwillard, PA: Safe Harbour Press, 1992.

Ward, Jandl H, Thorman, Jan, and Cole, Katherine H, (comps.) *Historic Railroad Stations: A Selected Inventory*. Washington, DC: National Park Service Pub. No. 124, 1974.   <

< 79 >

< Train Stations >

Index

< 80 >